THE THRESHOLD

THE THRESHOLD
The Forces of Techno-Materialism
and the Struggle for Humanity's Soul

Kingsley L. Dennis

AEON

First published in 2025 by
Aeon Books

British Library Cataloguing in Publication Data

A C.I.P. for this book is available from the British Library

ISBN-13: 978-1-80152-185-7

Typeset by Medlar Publishing Solutions Pvt Ltd, India

www.aeonbooks.co.uk

Corruptio optimi pessima

"The corruption of the best is the worst"

CONTENTS

ACKNOWLEDGEMENTS

I'd like to express deep thanks to my friend and musical partner Moin Mohamed Islam for all the chats we've had over the last few years, and the music we've made together. The creative act of transforming ideas and concepts into musical journeys has been a healthy and enjoyable one. Our musical journey—as Dr. Dennis & Dedfela—has been one of safe surfing the sacred among the profane. And if you would like to learn more—check out our music online.

NOTE FROM THE AUTHOR

There is always darkness before the light. That is how it is—or must be. I say this now, before the reader ventures further into this text. There is a dark tunnel that we must pass through before emerging into a revealing light. There is some dark philosophy ahead in these pages. It may seem oppressive at times. Yet awareness and attention demand their own recognition of the road ahead. We owe it to these faculties, and to ourselves, to be forewarned of the potential landscapes that await the unsuspecting traveller, who takes the populist path, where the dragons lie in wait. If you intuit, or even see, the sign—*Here Be Dragons*—you will then have the foresight of knowing where you will step. If you walk ahead with the spark of light inside you, then you will have nothing to fear from the following trail of musings. Walk on.

Approaching the threshold

At present mankind is undergoing an evolutionary crisis in which is concealed a choice of its destiny

—Sri Aurobindo

Everything is changing, but the most significant event of our time is a deep, decisive transformation in the faculties of the human being ...

—Rudolf Steiner

If we are to see where we are going (or may be heading), we first need to examine, and acknowledge, where we presently are. And humanity is presently undergoing an evolutionary crisis and is in the process of forgetting what it means to be human—what the human connection means—and what is the genuine path forward for the human species. To the casual observer, it would seem that this bipedal carbon-based species has lost its way. The cosmos has come to mean nothing to us—just an "empty space" somewhere "out there" that one day we may colonise. The world we know of and the "reality" it provides for us has become a chaotic playing field full of our projected fantasies, desires, and all else in between. There is little or no eternal or Absolute that we feel connected to, that moors us or equilibrates us within this rumbling sea. The sacred, silver umbilical cord within the soul of humanity lies shrouded in dust. Humanity is largely unable to find its intrinsic value and worth and looks away from the eternal questions. In fact, there is no sense of the *authentic eternal* within the human condition, and the path of destiny is regarded as a concrete paved multi-lane highway going nowhere in particular. Modern history is looked upon as a road to nowhere, scattered with the discarded trinkets, charms, and totems of both decadent and impoverished lives. Humanity, in short, is unable to perceive its own greatness. It is losing its collective soul to the titans of industry, commerce, and meta-materialistic nihilism. In 1957 the American Catholic monk Thomas Merton published the following statement:

> The world of our time is in confusion. It is reaching the peak of the greatest crisis in history. Never before has there been such a total upheaval of the human race. Tremendous forces are at work, spiritual, sociological, economic and not least of all political. Mankind stands on the brink of a new barbarism, yet at the same time there remains possibilities for an unexpected and almost unbelievable solution, the creation of a new world and a new civilization the like of which has never been seen. We are face to face either with Antichrist or the Millennium, no one knows which.[1]

At the time of Merton's statement (in the 1950s), the end of the century's "Millennium" appeared as the potential antidote to the machinations of the Antichrist and its deepening materialism. Merton foresaw a "threshold moment" on the horizon only that he phrased this in the dating of his time. Humanity was eventually able to pass the marker of the third millennium, yet this did not resolve the situation but only prolonged its present momentum.

The postmodernists and the transhumanists would perhaps both alike call out that humanity is now entering into the stage and state of the post-human. Yet they would no doubt regard this as a philosophical and technological stage respectively. Metaphysically speaking, humanity is experiencing the liminal state of the "post-human" only in so far as we have drifted from any transcendental centre that keeps us connected to a greater, cosmic reality beyond the constricted limitations of the purely physical. We may be experiencing the post-human in that we are becoming splintered from the *essential* that makes us truly human.

We are certainly not past it yet; rather, we are teetering on the edge of a dangerous cliff. However, it is exactly at such teetering points—places of hazard—that great leaps are taken, and where significant thresholds are passed. The denial of the eternal is also the devolvement of the present. Perhaps, at this stage, there is nowhere else to go except further denial, or an unsuspecting form of rejuvenation, restoration or, one might be bold enough even to say, the revelation of apocalypse?

A present cycle of human time is coming to a close. According to the second law of thermodynamics, everything is moving towards final collapse, or ending, through entropy. That is, through the gradual decay and dispersal of energy, all material systems eventually move from order into disorder, chaos, and breakdown. These are the laws that appear to govern physical processes in the external world. All physical bodies, systems, and cultures go from birth to decay. Whatever has emerged into physical manifestation has already begun to die. And it is in these latter times of decay where deteriorated forms of life are most prominent. Or, to give it a spiritual-religious context, where the forms of evil are most manifest. According to philosopher Charles Upton, "The nadir of human spiritual receptivity must, according to the doctrine of many spiritual traditions, manifest not simply as the disappearance of spirituality, but as the satanic counterfeit of it."[2] It is perhaps because of this that there has presently arisen so much mythological and sociocultural significance concerning the "End Times"— from the Bible's *Revelation of St. John* to indigenous prophecies and their calendars, ancient legends, catastrophe cycles, and more. Within the cycles of history, as envisioned by the human eye, there are peaks and troughs within cultures and civilisations; redresses and mini-restarts and resets; and various revivals and renewals. Each generation looks back at its own recent history and sees the dark times it has left behind. Within each generation there are heroic struggles and catastrophic failures. There is corruption, death, and forms of insanity within every epoch of history. Why would this one be any different, we may ask? Every culture has had its hidden and visible demons and angels, djinns and afrits, saviours and demolishers. And yet, I repeat: a present cycle of human time is coming to a close. It may be the "Big One" or it may be one of a series of redresses along the spiral of evolutionary time. We shall see.

As we stand upon the shore and look out to the far reaches of the sea, we notice a wave coming. It is gathering pace. Yet we are not able to measure its size or perceive its potential impact: we only know that it is there, and it is coming our way. And without any intervention from beyond the physical realm, it will arrive to this shore at some distinct moment. Each wave begins from a point of origin and accumulates greater energy or order as it ripples and rolls across the ocean. And at some point, as it nears the shore, this great watery edifice comes crashing down into a cacophony of chaos and dissolution. It is but the same cycle again and again. This is how the shore receives its nutrients. Each wave that crashes upon the shore brings new minerals from its depths. Sometimes, a stage within the current world is demolished; other times, a world age comes to its close as a marker for the new to emerge.

The climax of despair indicates that a breakthrough is imminent. Yet any genuine breakthrough will not first emerge upon the exoteric level; that is, upon the external stage of physical manifestation. These are the false revolutions of hope that only return to the same game. All revolutions are co-opted and merge once again into the fold of external historical events. The only real breakthrough can be upon the esoteric level—through the realm of the metaphysical and how this is transmitted through the material domain. Within these dimensions we are influenced through the morphing and pulsations of time and space. We can sense this through our own life experiences; when we are calm and relaxed, space seems more real to us than time. Just as in meditation when time falls away and we exist within a realm of space. And yet, when we are anxious or restless, we sense the onrush and the deliverance of time. Right now, in our world scenario, we feel time not just slipping by but rushing past us frantically, the wind blowing against our ears. Everything is moving fast now; and space is being eliminated. In virtual spaces especially, where avatars mock our personhood, space is eliminated entirely as it is substituted by the false space of the digital. And communications zip around our heads mimicking a new realm of the demolished time of the instantaneous. There may be a Singularity coming, yet it is less likely to be the one that the tech-transhumanists are eager for. Yet before we reach that threshold, we must be cognisant of the fact that the lowest forms of manifestation are likely to be witnessed as they are to be displayed and/or exposed during the final part of this cycle.

Many people are currently feeling and experiencing the exhaustion of chaos; the exhaustion that arises before the coming threshold looms. Yet, as it is said in Psalm 23:4, "Even though I walk through the valley of the shadow of death, I will fear no evil." And it is somewhat like that valley which we are today traversing, in order to reach (and hopefully pass) the entry into a different era of the human life experience. First, though, the shadow and the void—the *separation*—must be experienced on a collective level before any closure can be expected. This is perhaps what has been somewhat mythically referred to in various guises as "Hell". Although for myself, I would deem this as a state of non-realisation and/or not-being. And these are the extremes of a polarity that faces humanity within its current manifestation in this dimension. The human being is having to face the expressions and manifestations of the absence of being. Yet this may not necessarily be a state or space of *non-being* for this is often recognised as a spiritual state that transcends the realm of the senses. In these times where we witness the rising of the machinic impulses and its adherents, which shall cause discomfort for humankind, the absence of being is put forward in these pages as a *not-being*. It is human to ask questions about our "being" and essence. Without questioning the very "beingness" of our nature we are falling short and doing a disservice to our responsibility as a human being. That is why, surrounded by an onslaught of mechanicalness and automation, I refer to the encroaching state of not-being. This state, and the dilemmas it poses, suggest an uncomfortable road. However, it is never a smooth road on the approach to a threshold. It is more like a cobbled walkway.

* * *

This book deals with what is ahead for humanity if it collectively chooses the wrong path—the negating path—or what may be called the *path of denial*. That is, a rejection of the genuine path of the human spirit and its capacity to develop and evolve along its corresponding trajectory. Within the pages of this book, I examine the machinations of techno-materialism, and the issues facing humanity in this turbulent phase of its collective journey. Some of the material is justifiably dark, for it reflects the shadows that are presently in play all around us. Yet, dear reader, be heartened, for where there are shadows there will always be the origin of light. Before there can be revelation, the atrocities behind the curtain must be recognised for what they portray—and also for what they portend for a future we do not wish to arrive to. By showing the path of not-being and evolutionary stagnation, it is my hope that I will have sufficiently shone a light upon the great nobility of the human species, and the authentic choices we need to make to enable that nobility into expression. Now, the reader must bear with me—we have work to do.

Notes

1. Thomas Merton, *The Silent Life* (London: Burns & Oates, 1957), 173.
2. Charles Upton, *Legends of the End: Prophecies of the End Times, Antichrist, Apocalypse, and Messiah from Eight Religious Traditions* (Hillsdale, NY: Sophia Perennis, 2005), 13.

CHAPTER ONE

The external gaze of the global shadow

... what has no parallel is this gigantic collective hallucination by which a whole section of humanity has come to take the vainest fantasies for incontestable realities ...

—Rene Guenon

What has materialised as our so-called "modern world" can no longer be seen or considered as a "breakthrough" but as in a breakdown mode, for the external outreach of globalising forces and powers has brought humanity to a threshold. It is a threshold—a crisis point—of meaning and future orientation. It is, in other words, a period of existential crisis for the human race. Rene Guenon, in the above opening citation, refers to this predicament as a "gigantic collective hallucination". He is right in a general way. And yet, within the human collective, there is no longer a shared hallucination but a fragmentation of hallucinatory visions. The reality construct which we inhabit has become a fragmentary, splintered landscape. It is a scarred terrain upon which can be seen the pockmarks of a dried materialism. Dried—and shrivelled—for it is absent of any genuine spiritual or transcendental component. Deepening material forces have pushed, and continue to push, out across the planet, forcing themselves upon a largely organic environment.

Intelligence is being substituted by intellect—a force utilised to act on matter to produce utilitarian ends. And science, by and large, is an area that has been developed into an industry and with industrial applications. Science has become invested as a driving force behind the military-tech-industrial complex. Intellect, devoid of a connection to an inner, reflective world, is heavily used in the manufacture of what can only be termed "artificial objects". It is a turn away from the metaphysical, towards the categorisation of the "other" or "meta", and a diminishing of the perceptual spectrum. It is an outward gazing eye of intellect that is inwardly blind to intuitive insight. And yet it is perfectly suited to an era of machinic advancement. Genuine intelligence is being subtly replaced by its lesser cousin—the intellect.

Parallel to the outward gaze of the intellect lies a continued onslaught and assault against those aspects deemed as organic—the bodily, agricultural, and environmental domains where carbon reigns as a vital and necessary component. Those elements vital to organic life are being demonised, targeted for eradication, and also monitored and monetised. The administrations of control are hijacking utilitarian narratives to underpin the pseudo-morality of a modernised, globalised world order. It is a morality that has inverted essential human values (as I discussed in my previous book, *The Inversion*). A corporatised, oligarchical civilisation has formed as an abnormal bodily cell from the perspective of essential human values, and yet it is setting itself up as the controlling world order for the future trajectory of a globalised civilisation. Here, the tumour is metastasising, and it is "cancerising" the many cells within the organic host body.

Any notion of progress is now defined within terms of material development, regardless of whether this development has a corresponding set of values and ethics. The concept of "progress" has become interchangeable with the notion of "civilisation" as if the two naturally go together. And any arguments against this will be considered as coming from a Luddite or "primitive" perspective. The modern idea of progress can be seen as a relatively recent invention based upon a material paradigm rather than one of inner growth and conscious evolution. The word itself—"civilisation"—only entered our lexicon within the last couple of centuries. Again, it is a perspective that belongs to world creation, or *worlding*, that fits into an agenda of global scale. Western, especially European, expansion in the eighteenth and nineteenth centuries took on the mantle of "civilisation" to export it upon less so-called "developed" or less industrialised cultures. The notion of civilisation from Western eyes was thus tinged from its beginnings as a hierarchical and colonising scheme, with high value placed upon westernised notions of superior intellect and empirical science. Corporatised ideas of civilisation then are clearly tied with a paradigm of materialism and material progress—the very thing now epitomised by AI deep machine learning, algorithms, and digital systems. Furthermore, the mentality of the globalised "collective civilisation" of today is a mass suggestibility—a programmed mentality.

The Russian American sociologist Pitirim Sorokin noted that societies could be recognised according to their "cultural mentality". These, he wrote, could be distinguished between "ideational", where reality is primarily considered as spiritual and immaterial; "sensate", where truth is seen as material and to be gained through materiality; and "idealistic", which is a synthesis of the two. Past crises to hit the human realm were responded to according to the type of cultural mentality at the time. And for centuries, human society, cultures, and civilisations have had a religious and/or spiritual base or framework of one type or another. This does not mean that such cultures were predominantly religious but that they had a religious underpinning and organisational order. People overcame crises at the same time as believing in some form of religious framework—they believed in their god(s) even if they didn't know exactly what it was that they believed in. They just harboured some form of religious/spiritual worldview that aided them when it was necessary. Yet in more recent times, atheism has crept into cultural programming as if better suited to an industrialising worldview based upon a paradigm of material progress. The idea of a divine Source has been substituted by the forces of material progress: a randomised reality where the survival of the fittest is based upon who can imprint their will most strongly upon the materially malleable environment. As we shall see in later chapters, this has proven to be an ally in the transhumanist narrative, where technology has replaced divine order. Institutionalised religion has befallen the sins of corruption, and faith has been diverted into online metafusions of digital fantasy. Within this profusion of fragmented realities has arisen the psychological and emotional egregore (psychic entity) of nihilism. The Absolute has been removed from the reality paradigm and in its place dark matter, empty space, and meaningless has filled the vacuum. A global order is emerging, orchestrated from the shadows by an elusive and nefarious empire of elite hands, which in Sorokin's terms is primarily sensate in nature and design. And this, I would posit, is the crux of humanity's existential crisis.

* * *

The global shadow being cast across the planet is rewriting the historical narrative by attempting to create the illusion that a westernised Anglo-American based empire is being demolished and replaced with a more equitable multi-polar sibling of beneficial governance. And yet, as Herbert Marcuse warned us decades ago, the free election of masters does not abolish either the masters or the slaves. The brother of a "beneficial multi-polar world order" is the behemoth of Moloch in a new historical disguise. Within this reconstructed historical framework, any notion of the "human spirit" is now polarised into a mentality of medieval theology or rebranded through the corrupt corporate practices of commercial well-being, feelgood factors, and online guruism, etc. Within this dry, intellectualised, external gaze of progress and economic development there is virtually no space, no access for development upon a perceptual and intuitive level. Within today's material systems, structures, and institutions, inner growth is housed within life coaching sessions, managerial training, positive psychology, motivational retreats, and other economically certified courses. Within this abusive environment of the spirit, the worst pseudo-mystical extravagances are manifesting, from sexually abusive cults such as the US-celebrity sponsored sex cult Nxivm to the sexual and psychological assaults of Tibetan Buddhist Sogyal Rinpoche. The path to illumination has long been lingering on the borders of cruel madness. We may say that a hybrid form of "neo-spiritualism" has morphed out from the twentieth-century trend in pseudo-spiritual materials and teachings. A form of "syncretism" has arisen where the modern person is plied with a mix of materials—a "pick n mix" style of self-teachings for a heady homebrew recipe of modernist mysticism. This largely westernised mentality has become the model for a global psyche that is scattered in many directions, fragmented and splintered. This materialist approach to metaphysics is a mutation through the mutilation of materials.

It seems that the natural order of things has been cruelly reversed within this global world order. I have spoken before on how this current reality can be said to be an "anomaly" as it is not in correspondence or aligned with universal resonance. And when things come out of alignment and resonance for too long, a sharp jolt of realignment may be necessary. Yet such drastic realignments are not committed solely through the systems and structures of the physical world—such as through economics and/or geopolitics—but are also beyond these material gestures. It is for this reason that recognition and/or acknowledgement of a metaphysical foundation to existence is, in my view, critical. For without this, all comprehension of the changes and/or upheaval will be met with an empty materialistic response. And this will hit the human being even harder than necessary. In approaching the threshold, the boundary between crisis and revelation, a person's state of being will decide how, and to what degree, such events and encounters are received and experienced. Much of modern human society displays a "spirit of negation" in that it places everything into systems and structures that, by their nature, have limited or no place for transcendence. This is a contradictory position to universal laws of ongoing transcendence and evolvement. Globalised modernity, especially, negates consciousness as primary (as "before matter") and this negation is in part responsible for the inverted dominance of the materialistic narrative. Rational knowledge systems lack a transcendental impulse; as such, they are incomplete and only a mirroring, a shadow, of more complete reality. Human cognition and perspectives are conditioned, under a modern approach, to be rationalistic and linear. Anything that is not linear is seen as chaotic, random, unpredictable, and thus something to be feared or contained. This then forms blinkered perceptions that are constrained by external artefacts, just as horses are tacked with blinkers that reduce their vision. Humans are restrained or fastened not by physical blinders but by programmed ones. Each individual, then, is faced with the choice of whether or not to maintain their own immunity against cognitive and perceptual decline and degradation.

Within the external gaze of the global shadow, physical comforts and conveniences are seen as the epitome of progress. As such, mechanisation that can provide a short-cut to these conveniences, and which can elevate modes of comfort, are considered a sign of humanity's progress. The extreme extension of this linear view sees the rise of the digital domains, the metaverses, as being the pinnacle of physical convenience. Less and less will participants realise the contrary discomfort of the physical body, strapped in a chair with its headset, as this posture becomes "normalised" into routine. The ideal of modern progress being fostered upon an uncertain world is being sold through the saviour of illusionary domains and the relegation of the natural, organic world to the mechanical impulse that constitutes the control regimes and archi-tectures of oppression of the artificial, regulated realm.

The programmed mass mindset is attracted to popularism and to "mass event" information and stimulation. Populist information is almost totally serviced through sponsored propaganda. Yet this popu-larised form of propaganda comes at a price—the detriment of truth. By making such information "accessible to all", this means diminishing it to the lowest possible denominator. For these "truths" are not "Truth" at all, but information bites "piecemealed" together. Popularised knowl-edge (aka, information) contains nothing of the transcendent. In fact, mass popularism is a hollowing out of transcendent aspects—an empty shell serving the whole. This is in part responsible for the deformed mentality that passes for modern intelligence. This is not meant as a highbrow statement but rather the recognition that what passes for edu-cation these days is a form of programmed information and behavioural conditioning. Due to this early-stage programming, the mind becomes used to fixed patterning, and is flexible only to a degree, yet not far enough. The arrival of new thought patterns can cause an irritability—a mental irascibility—that brings on a reluctance for changing ideas. Yet change is upon us now more than ever. If we are not able to question our own beliefs, opinions, and ideas, then we are vulnerable to the increas-ingly sophisticated mind programming mechanisms of the encroach-ing global order. Approaching the threshold—or any threshold for that matter—means being prepared for experiencing the new, or that which has previously been beyond the periphery of perception.

Let us be warned that the surface-dwelling intellect is drawn to matter, materiality, and physicality more than it is to the non-visible domains. The globalising mindset that has been fostered upon humanity, over the past few decades especially, is creating a mental entanglement into mate-rial life. Globalisation is not of goods and services only—it also belongs to a programming of the human mind. A globalised mindset aims to be a homogenised one, where diverse thinking patterns are gradually reduced to a mass denominator thinking—a collective mob mentality. Such a standardised model of thinking is then easier to control and manipulate. Sovereign thinking, the once bastion of free will, becomes mechanical and outwardly steered through censorship parading as a politically correct "cancel culture". We end up self-censoring our own minds for fear of not fitting in with the mass mentality. Through this, a person becomes imprisoned in their life as they act as both jailor and prisoner—they have thrown away their own keys.

The only modality of life is change and constant renewal. And this also includes our thinking patterns and modes of perception. As humanity approaches its threshold—a looming cultural event horizon—we are compelled to choose between a global indoctrination or a species initiation. As it stands, the present incarnation of human civilisation does not include any transcendent order and few potentials for it. Because of this, the general individual today, caught up within the funfair of a heightened entertainment culture industry, has no knowledge, or even interest, in metaphysics and a transcendent order—they are only aware and/or interested in those aspects that belong to the rational order. Yet metaphysical understanding—a perception of events beyond the normal ken—does not depend on or operate through logic, linearity, or current timescales. The current reality narrative that is being pushed through the materialistic global order is in complete disorder. It has broken away from humane principles, morals, values, and ethics. A restoration of human civilisation is necessary—and thus, a threshold is necessary. Elements of calculated intervention and control have trespassed across the world in the name of a new global order. It is a carefully managed commercial and psychological intrusion into as many territories as possible. This reprogramming and recalibration of human life has attempted to eradicate any notion of a suprasensible realm. Such notions have been pushed further and further to the periphery and even disparaged through such terms as the occult, fantastical, superstitious, or phantasmagorical. The relation to a transcendental reality has been lost through the encroachment of a worldview that sees the superiority of materialism and the quantifiable—the realm of mechanistic life that now fully supports the acceleration of inorganic, artificial forms of intellect. Science has penetrated matter to its depths—into the quark and neutrino of existence—and believes it has mastered the very foundations of life. This materialistic hubris has given modern humanity a false sense of progress and a two-dimensional view of human evolution. This skewed understanding has also created an inverted sense of scientific and industrialised supremacy; and this comes at the expense of the transcendental impulse. Present human civilisation is undergoing an existential crisis.

These existential times

That which is most necessary to us now has become more hidden and inaccessible. The inward gaze—the inner realisation of one's connection to the Absolute—has become translated into seemingly obscure symbols, myths, and secret cults. This is another form of commercialisation: the commercialisation of secrecy and mystique. These practices only serve to satisfy the lowest elements of human psychological needs by feeding the so-called "spiritual" through the material side of curiosity and greed. Taken to the extreme, this continual reliance upon the external, the material, will force human evolutionary development into a suspension: a "state of dissolution from which it is impossible to emerge otherwise than by a cataclysm, since it is not a mere readjustment that is necessary at such a stage, but a complete renovation".[1] Disorder and confusion will come upon the world in a way that dramatises a global solution through an all-encompassing world order. The gravity of the situation should not be left to go unrecognised, for the endings of old worlds will foreshadow the beginnings of a new. Yet as the following chapters will describe, a form of what I call "pure technicity" will be pushed forth that aims to consolidate a "will to technology" instead of a "will to purpose". The drive towards progressive materialisation indicates a new cycle we do not wish to go down, for it will drown out almost entirely the suprasensible worlds—the supra-consciousness—from coming through into this realm (which is necessary for the next stage of planetary and human evolution).

The more that human beings give their autonomy to a technologically driven world (managed by a technocratic elite), the more they shall become slaves for they will have moved away from their inner transcendental impulse. The more that human civilisation drops into and is absorbed into an architecture of artificial construct, the further silenced are the finer realisations of the sacred order. We become dazzled, and entertained, by the multiplicities of material life at the expense of the higher principle of unified perception, cognition, and consciousness. Our perceptual vision is broken down into fractals, so that we attach externally to the increasing quantity of abstract distractions and thus diminish the quality of inward reflection and conscious awareness. Time is running out to awaken to the situation, before the perceptual entrapment has suddenly mutated into a physical one as well. And the reality construct of the entrapment shall be a profane one. In truth, there is no actual "profane realm" as all realities exist as manifestations from the Absolute. Yet the snare here, in this case, is that the reality construct shall be a domain for the profane point of view to be dominant. And this, at the bottom line, is a realm of ignorance. A realm closed off from the recognition of sacred influences and the potentials, and parameters, of transcendental development. A realm where imagination is controlled according to alignment with a machinic-intellect environment within an algorithmic architecture of expression. An individual's ideas shall be claimed as their own, for there will be no recognition for the allowance of inspirational influences from beyond the material brain. Notions of "the beyond" shall be fantasy waiting to be colonised by material possibilities—just as dreams of space were colonised by metallic constructs and moon mineral mining.

That which is not the product of the human or machine mind will just not exist. Knowledge will be classified as those ideas workable into empirical findings. Anything outside the human-machine intellect will be an error. The great Gnostic "error" shall have been consumed by the very artificial construct it was once warning us against. And all residual memory of these variables in the program will have been erased—and subsumed—by the very program now running. There shall be nothing recognised beyond the horizons of the external gaze. For us, reality will remain a bubble where the membrane is non-visible, and all relative truths are tightly kept within its domain. Only the gatekeepers (perhaps now machinic intellects) will know of the other dimensional realms, and yet such knowledge will be concealed from the inhabitants of the enclosure. Everything will have been reduced to a "sensible order". An order expanded through the "sensible" augmentation and merger with machinic interfaces, digitally rendered and algorithmically ordained. The new priests of the high castle will be the gods of artificial intellect who can interface with the quantum soup of the reality program. The human individual will no longer be wishing to climb Jacob's Ladder but will be content to voyage into meta-innerspace. Truth as an Absolute will become a residual memory held by the dying elders—the last ones to remember campfires and starlight.

It will become increasingly difficult for the higher influences arriving to this reality to reclaim humanity's evolutionary lineage as, according to the developmental law, the "higher cannot proceed from the lower, because the greater cannot proceed from the lesser".[2] Genuine developmental influences must come from a realm that is, using our terms, higher or beyond. The influences for higher development must be allowed to flow into our domain from a realm beyond. If they are cut off, then development within this reality construct is limited. And this limitation shall be fixed by material parameters. Technology cannot go beyond these limitations for it too is a manifestation of the material construct. True and genuine development is sanctioned by that which is *beyond* in order to reach down the ladder to assist in the climb. Our tools are with us, here in this reality, yet the impulses must come to activate us. The reversal of this universal order is when temporal, phenomenal power (of the senses) seeks independence from Absolute authority.

As I describe in the following chapters, the current trends vying for dominance in these times are pushing the human condition to become fundamentally out of synch with its natural, organic abode. It is a deeply materialistic drive towards a profane reality that augments the senses into perceiving a spectrum of enclosure (the "profanity"). As we walk, stumble, or transcend towards a looming civilisational threshold, we race against an impending enclosure against the developmental human future. The mechanistic forces of materialism seem intent on gaining dominion over this reality domain for the foreseeable future (however long that will be). And yet we know that matter itself is a divisive element for it overshadows the meta-physical—that which is beyond the physical—and clouds the senses away from the magical and onto the calculable and quantitatively mundane. In this, humanity has an adversary. It is a force, or range of forces, that persist in maintaining what I have referred to in my previous book as the *inversion*.[3] In this, our known reality construct is upside down and fosters the spirit of nega-tion and subversion. It marks the descending arc in an opposing direc-tion away from the influences of the Absolute. It is an *infernal* path that seeps deeper into the entanglements of a beguiling and often bedazzling perceptual reality where the senses are technologically stimulated into further rungs of the artificial kaleidoscope.

The future speaks to us in a hundred signs, or so said Friedrich Nietzsche. For starters, the signs of our future can be towards a *beingness* or a *not-beingness*. And from there, we shall take the next steps. First, we delve into the path of pure technicity and the will to technology.

Notes

1. Rene Guenon, *The Crisis of the Modern World* (Hillsdale, NY: Sophia Perennis, 2004a), 17.
2. Rene Guenon, *The Crisis of the Modern World* (Hillsdale, NY: Sophia Perennis, 2004a), 73.
3. See *The Inversion: How We Have Been Tricked into Perceiving a False Reality* (Aeon Books, 2023).

CHAPTER TWO

Pure technicity and the will to technology

The future speaks in a hundred signs even now
—Friedrich Nietzsche

Human life is currently experiencing a "re-tuning" and this is forming part of the mutation or a social-cultural-techno hybrid whose attunement to the human condition is now fundamentally out of synch. Technology now heralds a marker for our species split, rather than as a tool of cooperation for which it was once proclaimed. The need for alliance and cohesion is still there—a desperate need and deep longing— yet it is being usurped by both a human and a machinic urge for greed and power that lays bare the present playing field upon which humanity tentatively treads. The pathways of human thinking, the filaments that collectively make up a consciousness field, are being tampered with so that human minds are being deprogrammed from the inside out. The collective body of humanity is being organisationally steered and programmed into the path of automation—the *robosapiens*. This is the path of "not-being", and stands contrary and/or parallel to the path of the human "being". Laboratory blinkered minds are attempting to understand technologies in a technological manner, rather than from the human perspective. Humans are projecting into technology their limitations of understanding and perception, while projecting onto it an "otherness" that is not like us. It is not so much the technical that daunts us but that we are not yet prepared for where this trajectory may take us. Our minds are still scrambling for comprehension and knowledge while we give suck to a new breed of entities. The paradox of our predicament is nothing other than the blindness of our unpreparedness that underwrites our future vision. This is the "hauntology" of our times, as we are influenced and driven by those spectres of ideas, dreams, and wandering imaginations that are not yet physically present and yet which may still bite us.

Upon the horizon may be a future constructed out of immense social-cultural divisions—rulership and servitude—that unfold a "world-scape" of pure technicity. The logic of a disunified mind creates its own socio-techno matrix of entrapment. Humans are being positioned—or rather, set up—to be the agents for the greater unfolding of this "pure technicity". By pure technicity, I mean the reliance of humanity upon the range or systems of technology—the techno-ecosystem. The danger here is that this new "outer body" for humanity takes the human being on an evolutionary pathway further into external bodies and systems and away from the inner essence. Our technologies become the human exoskeleton, further stunting the growth of the inner kernel. We lose our centre of gravity. We become appendages, travellers, external pilgrims upon someone else's journey. We do not pass through John Keats' "Vale of soul-making" but instead skip through the scrapyard of evolutionary dead ends.[1] Let us ask the question: what is the essence of technology?

The machinic impulse races ahead for the quantification of all things. It arranges, sorts, organises, plans, predicts, programs, and finally, executes the programming. It does not seek the source of its existence. It builds yet it has no *being*. If technicity becomes our destiny, we lose the magic and mystery that lays within our central core. The techno-ecosystem will reshape the environment for all sentient life. There will be available space for a form of the human body (most probably a modified body), yet will there be room for *beingness* or for cosmically attuned vital forces? This shall be the preparation for a technologically induced terraforming of the planet Earth (see Chapter Six).

We need to consider technology as unravelling a mystique and not as an artificial intellect for organisation and convenience. Humanity first needs to step within before it can wholesomely step without. We're going about it all the wrong way. We are giving over the reins of the carriage to a mechanical beast before we, the passenger and driver, have even taken our driving test, let alone passed it. Humanity is becoming enclosed by the accelerated dominance of pure technicity so that Walter Benjamin's treatise *The Work of Art in the Age of Mechanical Reproduction* (1935) can now be updated as "The Art of Life in the Age of Digitally Rendered Perception". These technologies are now becoming the "technologies of disappearance" as certain elements of life are being eroded or made to disappear, including memory, identities, tangible possessions, sovereignty, privacy, freedom, reality … the list is long. Bodies become interfaces instead of sovereign vessels. This disappearance suggests that life now becomes a "hauntology" where things are no longer present but are represented only by their traces, the vestiges of their once-existence. Signals and signs of this historical hauntology have been pervasive throughout mainstream media with movies, television series, and books about zombies, the undead, and the myriad dystopian phantasmagorical wastelands. Perhaps this is part of the vulgarity that historian Oswald Spengler spoke about as signifying the end of a culture. Spengler announced a century ago that the Western world is ending, and we are witnessing the final season, the "winter", of its civilisational decline. The ghosts of our hauntological wasteland wander as spectres of distress. And these posthuman ghosts shall be our clones. We are becoming increasingly tethered to our digital life through an unseen data-ecosystem—this is the hauntology of our lives, to be "tethered" through non-visible yet very present gossamer strings of measured constraint and containment.

This is where we have arrived to as a species, messing with our own mutations, the "delirious spectacle of clonal propagation, genetic sequencing, organ farms, recombinant DNA, and artificial life-forms created out of the vivisectioning of plants, animals, and humans …".[2] These are the contorted visions of a biogenetic future that aims to persuade us it is a normal extension of the digital hand of pure technicity. The social engineering of our times is complicit with a micromanaged genetic engineering that splices the carbon body and fragile psyche of the human individual that is as yet unprepared for such interventions. We are now facing, inside and out, bodies without geographies, absent of identifiable landmarks—the scars and traumas of modified landscapes. The pervasive digital-tech ecosystem and new "cryptography of the body" is leading to a form of cultural trauma, enmeshed and fortified by the dynamics of chaos being unleashed upon the disarray of the modern world. Even the "postmodern" world now tiptoes on the precipice of the abyss:

> In these visions recombinant of transgenic bodies, phosphorescent skin, jellyfish monkeys, firefly organs, mutant fish, sterile hybrid seeds, cross-species organs, there was the awakening again of the siren-call of a society intent on its own suicide, celebrating its coming disappearance in the language of the genetic modification of the species.[3]

The infamous line from Friedrich Nietzsche comes to mind here where he said that if you gaze long enough into an abyss, the abyss will gaze back into you. This abyss is being formed by a merger, or a smothering, with the new technologies that are self-evolving within the human blind spot. We see them and yet we do not see them for what they are, as humans have adopted a specific blindsight within the void. Nietzsche warned us in advance of the "will to nothingness", that could form the new contagion, the unseen motor of an inherent annihilation impulse within humanity. There appears to be a hidden impulse within a certain segment of human society that wishes for species annihilation, or to germinate the genetic suicide seeds within us. The path to pure technicity is paved upon uncertain experimentation. As one cultural commentator put it: "In the sometimes utopian, always militaristic, language of technological experimentalism, 'not-being' finally becomes a world-historical project."[4] Is this project of "not-being" also part of, or the same thing, as our cultural annihilation? The technocratic "will to technology"—a dystopian form of immortal life—actually suggests this unsteady state of potential permanent annihilation.

Perhaps we should position ourselves so that technology is "not-being" and the human is, of course, the human "being". A technological destiny (and a political technocracy) is therefore a future of "not-being": it may be smart and clever, yet it shall be intellect only and not intelligence for it is forever smart but never soulful. The current "will to technology" only further deepens the metaphysical crisis in contemporary human culture (as I discussed in my earlier book *Healing the Wounded Mind*). If humanity is to endorse the technocentric "not-being" as the next evolutionary trajectory, then we may be setting up a destiny that arrives at the walled end of a dead-end street. To endorse "not-being" is nothing more than to declare ourselves—and the human species—as anti-life and, as such, as an alienated anomaly within the conscious mind of the cosmos. To choose "not-being" is ultimately to choose our oblivion.

We could perhaps declare this mind-scape as the metaphysics of the void (see Chapter Five). We may look back at ourselves through the haze of the universal gaze and deeply wonder … where did it all go? If humanity endorses "not-being" as its evolutionary stance of stagnation, then it has expressed itself through an act of "not-will". This reflects a lack of the sovereign self, a negation of the inner metaphysical drive, and a fall into mechanical existence. This is the automated rhythm of waking sleep, the human drone—the *humdrone*. The "humdrone" is the vacant being. A biological shell emptied of essence. Such individuals are like cracked eggs that propel themselves through life with the minimal use of their motor functions. The "not-will" is the very antithesis to the "will-to-truth". Such a will-to-truth is the overcoming of one's own social programming and conditioning, and the pathway to coming to terms with one's own truth by turning away from the dominance of the personality and towards one's essence. It is this essence that brings out the *beingness* as a counteraction against the "not-being" that is the energy that feeds the global technological engine. The technocrats are putting themselves out there as the new global gods of bio-digital mutation—yet it is we, the sovereign individuals, who are the technicians of the soul.

The technocratic jurisdiction of pure technicity—the downloading of culture, society, sex, and consciousness—is a newly vat-grown social matrix of *harvested* bodies and *modified* minds (the aesthetics of extinction). Here we now have the dichotomy, or the split, between potential human futures. The hyper-material machinic timeline that will label itself as "post human" will claim to have objectified matter and spirit (body and mind) into an assemblage of codified data that can be modified (i.e., mishandled) to suit controlling interests. And then there will be the metaphysical human future timeline that will seek transcendence beyond technology where (somehow) matter and spirit will have merged, transfused, into an extended consciousness that roams beyond the confines of the body. And yet, it must be wondered whether the human species as a mass, a collective, will ever be ready for the metaphysical, transcendental adventure. As the esoteric philosopher Gurdjieff put it: *Sleep is very comfortable, but waking is very bitter.* Most likely upon the horizon is an extension of the current trajectory where the hyper-material future will create an existential boredom because it will have severed humanity from its sense of contact with itself, and with an eternal Origin—an Absolute—that vitalises existence. The hyper-material human future inevitably seeks to abolish unpredict-ability and unknown potential for it is coded upon attaining precision, predictability, and a quantifiable domain. The dynamics of an unpre-dictable life is anathema to a technocentric world culture with tech-nocracy at its core. What the hyper-material kingdom seeks is to reign through its programmed operating principle—and a metaphysical per-spective threatens this program. What needs to be recognised is that we can be initiates to a metaphysically infused human future, or drones—*humdrones*—within a digitally rendered sociocultural exoskeleton.

The worst kind of oppressiveness is the one we do not even suspect. It is the type of oppressiveness that becomes normalised into the fabric of our lives; an ennui, apathy, unrecognised boredom that gets interpreted as a civilising existence within a will-less realm of soulless humanity. The pic-ture emerging here is of an unconscious yet "sentient" species that lives as a membrane upon the Earth (as its textured skin) yet lacking any organs of perception. There is no greater emptiness than an absence of *being*. An eco-system of pure technicity where dependence is a ubiquitous necessity can only demolish the presence of *beingness* or stifle it before it is even birthed within people. This is the premise of Aldous Huxley's *Brave New World* where vat-born babies are basically raised into programmable *humdrones*. The humdrones act as "swarm machines" in response to programmed orders. They infiltrate the social institutions, carry out orders, fill in the data boxes, and do the bidding of the unseen overlords (whoever they may be). The French theorist Jean Baudrillard claimed that new technolo-gies always begin with the disappearance of the real. The looming tech-horizon that stands before us is dealing with the disappearance of the real human being. As Baudrillard wrote: "… we are currently obliterating the traces of our existence, spiriting away the evidence for our sensible world … future 'humans' will have no navels ... we are already in the 'umbilical limbo'."[5] Baudrillard further reminds us that if it were not for appearances then the world would be a perfect crime. And this crime would perhaps be a technologically overdetermined society that imposes a linear view of history; an illusion of a "natural" progression that hides the cracking and splintering that produces, or offers, a bifurcation upon humanity's path-way. As it currently stands, the human species has entered upon the early stages of being "terrorised by code"—an agent of control that lies beyond any physical grasp and beyond calls for its culpability.

Humanity has arrived at a civilisational crisis point and we have yet to understand, in any fundamental way, what it means to live a life by "being" as opposed to "not-being". We are yet to recognise this difference, and this is a metaphysical apathy that is nudging our species into an existential riptide. The philosopher Hannah Arendt once described Western society's headlong rush into a technological future as a "process of annihilation" that stands upon the triumph of "not-being". What we as a sentient species now need to aspire towards is a heightened metaphysical consciousness that opens up a psychic connection to an extended mind and to contact with intelligence beyond the confines of the physical body. The contrary pathway to this is the "quantifiable self" that is the data flesh for the new amalgamated human-digital body (see Chapter Seven). The will to technology that represents the path to pure technicity seems determined to establish the external control of consciousness that is implicated within the networks of an artificial intellect that is more imprisoned than psychic. Any techno-induced "metaphysical architecture" of coded spaces is only "meta" in terms of a corporatised controlled domain where dependence is predicated upon detachment from the essential human *being* and from any genuine metaphysical, transcendental impulse.

The externalisation of self

One of the consequences of an increasingly modernised way of life is the perspective that humans live as separate nodes within an environment that is exterior to them. This gives rise to the imagined idea that machines are external nodes also, rather than being an assemblage or networked ecosystem of information. The pure technicity that faces us is not encased in a robotic shell, a human-looking android or replica. It is the ecosystem of a data-driven information architecture that communicates through a decentralised medium or "body". Similarly, it is this sociocultural assemblage that has given birth to the highly adaptive, complex organism of an artificial intellect. It is our spawn. And as such, it begins its infancy by inheriting our flaws. The machinic assemblage is not a single entity; it is a form of organism based upon algorithms and code of self-replication, auto-complexity, and machinic-evolvement. That is, like all other organisms, it has the potential to reproduce itself through networks of co-evolution, feeding off the data that we provide for it. It is the "social machine" that has actualised these potentials, and

humans seem to be, by and large, oblivious to the unfolding circumstances. Just as the human being is described as a machine, an automaton, so too can the machinic assemblage be viewed as an organ. It may
be that pure technicity, the reliance of humanity upon the techno-
ecosystem, is a wider part of a new social-machinic complex that feeds
into an overarching control world state where there is no going back.
The human being is a particle within this hybrid organ/organism. It is
the social realm that comes first for it is the breeding ground for all later
birthed systems and constructs. It is the human fantasy that gives birth
to such systems:

> The human fantasy is to devise a technological system so omni-
> scient that it nullifies the power of the future, transforming the
> universe into a perfectly administered megamachine of predictable
> outputs and calculable energies.[6]

The megamachine that lies ahead of us, and which has been in gestation over the past centuries of industrial growth, is morphing into an
amorphous-like artificial style of intellect that may not be susceptible
to the eroding forces of entropy that waylay organic humans.[7] While
humans shall wither and turn to dust, our digitised counterparts will
march on, developing and advancing with each deeply learned itera-
tion. And this scares us. And perhaps it should.

   In short, we don't know how evolution really works for it is something that is done to us, in the long term, and we can only make educated
guesses about it through the back-engineering of history. Yet evolution
cannot be contained—nor should it. In order to remain relevant, the
two-legged carbon-bodied human needs to develop also. And the only
long-term choice here is through an extension of perception, cognition,
and consciousness. We've always believed that technology functioned
as an extension of our own body and minds as we projected outwards
our desires, goals, wants, and intentions. The rise of the machinic-
artificial was a reflection of our own desires to control the world around
us. It is the exterior construct of the brain's left hemisphere as it sought
a partner to work through in its bid to grasp more power, control, and
order. Yet now this infantile state of the human condition has gone contagious as "our" machines are springboarding away from this foundation of human greed and paranoia—and expanding beyond this in a
way unknown to us. And the human being is getting left behind within

a viral reality of its own making. We have come face-to-face with our own questioning: what is to become of the human being? Is this the juncture—the *threshold*—that is fast approaching us and from which we cannot turn away or turn back?

The techno-forces that are programmed for control and human management are anti-evolutionary for they view everything as needing to be placed within a pristine order free from unforeseen and spontaneous stimuli. Life is now being turned into a procedure—a series of procedures—rather than a participation, a relation of correspondences. Now there is a machinic crusade for certitude, to be able to quantify and accredit, to categorise and data-stamp. A fully ordained technosphere will aim to keep humankind in a managed bubble, out of reach from such incalculable interventions. Opportunities for variation that often arise upon the scene, bringing with them the unexpected yet necessary energies for development, will be banished from such an artificial containment bubble. Deviation from the "new norm" is not required. This is the "not-being" of existence—a vacuum marooned species, immaculately stored in memory data banks rather than in bio-plasma, carbon-driven evolving bodies. French theorist Jean Baudrillard saw a possible end of human evolution upon the horizon as "In his arrogant desire to end evolution, man is ushering in involution and the revival of inhuman, biogenetic forms."[8] Scientific materialism is aiming for a technologically engineered life where genes are the building blocks to be spliced, diced, and digitally rearranged within a body. It is precision engineering, much like how you would construct a modern car. But bodies and real life are messy. We deal with germs and thousands of types of bacteria, as well as the cosmic bacteria and viral dust that lands on the Earth, our soil, and on us, throughout life. In fact, the human species, it is speculated, was the result of a panspermia impregnation from the cosmic heavens.[9] The underlying foundation to human life is its interrelation with everything else—except, perhaps, our rising machinic intellects.

The interplay with our technologies is like trying to find the most appropriate pivot that keeps a dynamic balance in play. Yet so far, this act of equilibrium is swaying hesitantly between various potential chaotic attractors. It is the inhuman futures that must concern us, as the future history of our noble species may likely be redefined (re-identified and re-gendered) so that we claim these futures as the "new human". We need to ask: what does it mean when voices start to call out for the post-human or the meta-human? And who are such voices representing?

* * *

As this book attempts to point out, all life is within a play (or various plays) of forces that impinge, contend, compete, oppose, struggle, and much more, upon the open playing field of the vital energies, frequencies, and vibrations that make up what we refer to as reality. The technological impulse is but one stratum within this interplay of vital forces. This mode can be said to be the machinic assemblage, or what I have called the machinic impulse.[10] The question is whether these forces now interpenetrating the human life experience can be transmuted and utilised in a transformative manner. First, I delve into the crises of our time, the shadow and void that feed upon separation, non-realisation, not-being, and the material forces of über-nihilism. These are the aspects of a negated reality that may well push humanity towards a threshold that is still to be decided.

Notes

1. "Call the world, if you please, 'the Vale of Soul Making'. Then you will find out the use of the world …. There may be intelligences or sparks of the divinity in millions—but they are not Souls till they acquire identities, till each one is personally itself." (In a letter of April 21, 1819 from John Keats to his other brother George).
2. Arthur Kroker, *The Will to Technology and the Culture of Nihilism: Heidegger, Marx, and Nietzsche* (Toronto, Canada: University of Toronto Press, 2003), 12.
3. Arthur Kroker, *The Will to Technology and the Culture of Nihilism: Heidegger, Marx, and Nietzsche* (Toronto, Canada: University of Toronto Press, 2003), 13.
4. Arthur Kroker, *The Will to Technology and the Culture of Nihilism: Heidegger, Marx, and Nietzsche* (Toronto, Canada: University of Toronto Press, 2003), 17.
5. Jean Baudrillard, *The Perfect Crime* (London: Verso, 2008), 23.
6. Keith Ansell Pearson, *Viroid Life: Perspectives on Nietzsche and the Transhuman Condition* (London: Routledge, 1997), 152.

7. See the work of Lewis Mumford in *The Myth of the Machine* (New York: Harcourt Brace, 1970).

8. Jean Baudrillard, *The Illusion of the End* (Cambridge: Polity Press, 1994), 84.

9. See the Panspermia Hypothesis; also, Directed Panspermia. See *Life Itself* by Francis Crick (New York: Simon & Schuster, 1981).

10. See my book *The Inversion: How We Have Been Tricked into Perceiving a False Reality* (London: Aeon Books, 2023).

CHAPTER THREE

Recombinants of the human condition

> *The materialism which has developed in the last few centuries has alienated people from true reality. Human beings have been sundered from it and have grown inwardly lonely. Most lonely of all are those who have become detached from life, torn from its living context, and are now related only to the arid machine … A wasteland now exists in human souls*
>
> —Rudolf Steiner

Whatever this transitioning period is about, or will consist of, it will ultimately be centred upon the core question of the human condition and its potential within the emerging recombinant environment. That is, how aspects of human society and culture will be broken down and recombined (reassembled) and what this means for the inclusion and participation of the human being. Perhaps one of the grandest obstacles that now stands in our path is the very way we are defining ourselves; also, how we comprehend the epoch we have been in, are currently in, and are moving towards. We are incessantly being told that we are in a "post" stage—post-modernity, post-human—and yet these terms are misleading. What is happening, as is the way of evolution, is that we are ceaselessly *becoming*. We are not "post" anything, least of all post-human.

This signals that the human being is finished, done with, kaput—and this is beyond short-sighted thinking. It is also extremely dangerous. People talk of the post-human and post-human futures without having known the potentials of the current human condition. This can only show how lost or untethered humanity is—lost in the byways of its infantile imagination, fed and fuelled by media-sponsored fantasies, billionaire greed, and social media mass psychosis. What it indicates, sadly, is that this way of thinking treats the latest stage of the human being as a model—a dummy, a shopwindow mannequin. It seems that Western culture especially is drifting; a "drift culture" that has left its tethered moorings (whether it be morals, religious-spiritual sensibilities, or a sacred connection) and is desperate for a new way of seeing, a more nuanced perception. Arthur Kroker, a Canadian writer on culture and technology, says: "The polar shift of perception required to navigate the fast, complex drift currents of the posthuman condition literally involves a new way of seeing, that is, seeing like a robot, a code-work, an artifact of artificial intelligence, a splice."[1] An indication that the human being is becoming obligated to shift its perceptions to see "like a robot", a "code-work", or an "artifact" in order to navigate the arising "posthuman" currents. These are the murky waters that now surround the ship of state (or the ship of fools?). These are the signposts—the "seductive exits to the posthuman future"—that are "over-coded, over-normalized, over-secured, over-mediated, over-measured", according to Kroker, and which are altering our current reality bubble. Or perhaps it should be said, our *reality wobble*.

Our present reality construct is receptive to the arrival of a rapidly accelerating technological component that will, in various ways, intervene with our bodies and minds in a way that is going to fundamentally alter modalities of human consciousness, cognition, and perception. And yet, very few people are even asking the inevitable question: to what end? Within such a "culture drift" we are failing ourselves in supplying the adequate answers, and in this we are entering the slipstream of a metaphysical struggle. This is the paradox where the seeming acceleration of life/time through technicity may bring many people into a fog of inertia. And this is likely to lead into an unrealised and indeterminate form of nihilism—a form of "über-nihilism" (see Chapter Four). Humanity is heading for an imminent threshold of recombination where alliances, bonds, and relations are stripped down in order to be remixed together with different components;

new coagulations and fusions that leave our existent morals and ethics in a vacuum. This pending state of the "remix" is the *parasocial* (alongside social), as in a parallel processing of social norms where a new "site of existence" is being created through the embalming of pure technicity, forming a *para-site* of existence. And that is what it is: the new techno-sphere is a parasite.

The technologically backed media and data-ecosystem is externalising the human nervous system (as was recognised in the 1960s by Marshall McLuhan) and exteriorising the human sensorium. In other words, it is thrusting us *outward*. The human being, in moving into this so-called posthuman pathway, is leaving behind its interior portal and living increasingly upon its exterior—what I refer to as a *skin-dweller*. If this continues, then we shall be disconnecting from the internal life (the inner sublime) that can take us past the next human developmental threshold; instead, humanity shall be delivered into an evolutionary void. This void may well be the difference between information and knowledge. The left-hemispheric nature of the human brain, which focuses on a target and narrows its perception to grasp it, has been dominant in our human cultures for centuries.[2] This is the sequential mode of information retrieval and analysis; and this is what I feel is adding to our culture drift. The rapid accumulation of data is becoming likewise a *data drift* within the digital ecosystem that is turning it into an information swamp. People are releasing so much data with all their online activity, social media posts, X-twitterings, videos, images, likes and dislikes, etc., that the algorithms and data-bots are sweeping it all up for their "food" and auto deep-learning from this. We are awash in data drift. Technology is always, in one form of another, performing psychic surgery upon the human nervous system (as Marshall McLuhan also first pointed out). We need to begin to seriously consider whether the construct of such a technological society—a technicity—has a "negative intent or being" inherent in its mode of function and mode of operation. This may be what Jean Baudrillard was referring to when he said that the perfect crime is the perfect cover-up. Nothing remains to be seen of the crime: it never happened. We don't perceive the "negative being" of technology because it simply isn't viewable—it hides within the cover-up of the not-being. The philosopher Hannah Arendt in her last book noted that in the future it is likely that everything will get subordinated to the preservation of a technocratic system, and the self-preservation of technique will bring about a nihilism of "not-being".[3]

By simply not-being ourselves, we shall have ushered forth the perfect crime of the human annihilation by not being present.

The act of being present is fundamental to the human being and how it perceives and makes sense of the world around; that is, its environmental context. For our world reality to unfold within human perception, individuals need to be "present"—we have to turn up with our presence, not just automatically or mechanically. Things of the world are not just static for us but "come into being" for us—they come into *presence*. According to psychiatrist and author Iain McGilchrist, it is the right brain hemisphere which functions for this "coming into presence". How life's experiences are perceived by us, and thus received, all depends on how a person is present to those impacts. And this act of *presence* requires that we exist through our human *beingness*. Quite simply, a mechanical device or "smart machine" does not have the same organic state of presence; furthermore, perception for an inorganic construct is not a participatory act of unfoldment. The confrontation between a "not-being" intelligence (non-presence) and a "being" intelligence (presence) now stands before us as never before. Along with human presence—the placing of perception onto the world—also comes the notion of attendance. As a human being, we need to "attend", to put our attention onto something that will shape it into being and meaning for us. Things have meaning in our life in accordance with the type of attention we put onto them. In this, it can be said that many people simply lack attention—we don't "attend" to circumstances in our life. In other words, we don't "turn up" when it is necessary. We may be physically there, yet from a cognitive and consciousness perspective, we are absent. Being attendant/attentive is how we meet something, how we have experiences in life. Reality, for us, is an unfoldment; and within this unfolding we also project our inner thoughts, desires, emotions, and more, onto it. This makes for the rich texture and depth of human experience. For a human being, attention is thus the disposition of consciousness. Yet for a machinic form of intelligence, attention is replaced by extraction, and any related meaning is gained through the extraction, accumulation, and the processing of data and information. The question that arises is what form of processing, and thus "intelligence", is going to be more evolutionarily suitable for the future. The human worry here, no doubt, is that the machinic form of intellect/intelligence is going to be more successful in the face of incoming changes. Or perhaps, these changes are going to be intentionally adapted to create an environment that has been selected for a machinic intelligence. This is a proposition that I discuss further in Chapter Six.

The sociocultural (and now electro-digital) environment is entangling the human being within forces that are compelling a mutation from the outside as well as within. As it stands, the current human is an embryo of what is to come—or what *can* become. The growth and development of the human being has never been a smooth or harmonious path; it has been a disjointed one, and at times treacherous. It has involved unexpected twists and turns, and some disastrous side journeys. Humanity is a work in progress, and that progress has always been a learning curve and not a walk in a flowery meadow. We've always learned by our mistakes (most of the time), even though we tend to often repeat them before the lesson sinks in. The human path develops in a spiral and often in response to particular feedback loops. It has been slow going most of the time. Yet there have been intervals also where a "shock" has occurred—an event or occasion—that creates the momentum for a jolt and a spurt forward. Often, such discord needs time to be internalised where it can be assimilated into our lives so we can utilise it for our further development, rather than being blocked by it. The human being is a porous creature. We are forever absorbing aspects, impacts, and residues from our environment and feeding off these. And so, the question is asked: are we teetering on the edge of such a "shock event" right now? And if we are, would we know how to benefit from it? For if humanity is not able to recognise the type of threshold that stands before it, then there is the possibility that it may pass the baton to the next runner before the race is done.

There is no next step without the further "becoming"—that is, internal development—of the human being; and at each moment it seems that humanity is facing yet another trial. It can be said, with good reason, that the human is a site of perpetual overcoming. And still, we must forge ahead. This perpetual overcoming is the constant experimentation that is the life of the human. And from the dawn of this human experiment there have been countless minds looking inwards and beyond, wondering if there is some great intelligence watching on and observing the grand experiment taking place within matter below. Life is a spectacle; and yet, somehow it is also sacred and profound at the same time in ways we are yet to fathom. Perhaps this is the "eternal return" that keeps our souls in a loop, repeating on and on until we can propel this material abode into a sacred realm. And opposed to this are the forces of ever-deepening materialism that are now forging the manacles of the "will to technology" and the implementation of a pure technicity over the flesh and bones of a blessed being. The struggle of being human persists. However, the religious-spiritual notion of the eternal return of souls can soon be substituted by the mechanical production and reproduction mechanisms that a machinic assemblage could put in place (especially for the younger generations). A hybrid body, or vessel, could be re-placed and constantly updated for recurring repeats of some form of incubating intelligence (see Chapter Seven). It sounds demonic, and perhaps it is, if driven by less than vital forces or non-evolutionary forces. What it comes down to is a necessary recognition and comprehension of the human condition. Especially now, when we are simultaneously stepping into a time/zone where recombinant forces are surrounding and engulfing the human being and probing it for future possibilities.

Humanity can transform its nature by inward compulsion or have its nature transformed by external forces. Both possibilities lead to different ends. We have managed to get thus far by carrying the notion that technology is an appendage to us, like an extra limb or added tool. We have failed to see it as a complex organism that can evolve and/or develop outside the limits of current human cognition. As one commentator put it: "History appears to have reached the weird point where it is no longer possible to determine whether technology as an extended phenotype is an expression of the desire of our genes or a sign of nature's cultural conspiracy."[4] Other voices view technology as a means to get past, and beyond, the human "blockage" that somehow sits in the way of further progress. It brings up the image of a whole squadron of dissenting humans sitting in the middle of the road as part of a sociocultural protest, like stopping traffic or something. Only that this is no ordinary road—it is the evolutionary pathway. And it is the encroaching army of AI bots with their deep learning whips that will override the blockage and clear the way forward. Human flesh and bones, and venerable mortality, is a burden to progress (some voices say). Out upon the wild frontier of the pioneers, only the machinic assemblage can now go where the mythological angels fear to tread. A worrying image.

Perhaps the first image we need to face up to is the imminent threshold in front of humanity where a new future beckons; a hybrid horizon upon which stands an altered condition of life. Will this be the recombinant human embroiled in the ecosystem of technicity—or will it involve a new phase in the psychic expansion and advancement of the human being? We are already being programmed with the info-propaganda of technicity where the integration with a machinic architecture seems clean, precise, efficient; while the carbon body stumbles, dribbles, and gets messy. This is why our lives are becoming more sanitised, so that we begin to look askance upon the "dirty" biological form. We are told to wash our hands regularly throughout the day; kill all bacteria and germs; avoid dirt, soil, and dust. In cleaning up our lives we are simultaneously killing off the immune system and losing our sovereign biological strength. We are being shown, it seems, the projected image of the human fantasy:

> The human fantasy is to devise a technological system so omni-scient that it nullifies the power of the future, transforming the universe into a perfectly administered megamachine of predictable outputs and calculable energies.[5]

The fantasy of technique and prediction over organic creativity is an infantile obsession that we can see was also propagated within the par-aphernalia of the previous industrial revolutions with their "efficient" modes of production. These precursors have laid the groundwork and crafted a sociocultural environment now responsive to a "Fourth Industrial Revolution" with its biotechnologies and human-machine integration.[6] As historian Lewis Mumford outlined more than half a century ago, human beings exist as pieces of a machine which they form alongside other elements such as animals, tools, systems, and motivations that all come together under the direction of a higher unity which he calls the *megamachine*. And in this, the human being cannot stand apart from, or easily exist separate from, this all-encompassing sociocultural construct of the megamachine.[7]

What is now becoming a fundamental question is that of the nature of intelligence. The vanguards of the AI race are competition-driven corporate behemoths, partly embedded or at least influenced by deep state intelligence-military agencies, that feed off the engineering wiz-ardry of tech-nerds living within a tech-utopia fantasy bubble. Great minds may well be immersed with discovering the fundamentals of both human and machine intelligence, yet this does not necessarily indi-cate that these "great minds" are themselves mature ones. High intellect does not denote deep intelligence any more than does intelligence suggest wisdom. There is clearly a demarcation between what stands for information and what is knowledge. These two categories also involve different forms of cognition as well as application. Information can only be utilised so far and has set limits. Knowledge allows for a much more expansive and nuanced understanding of both the context and its extended consequences. Unfortunately, modern human societies have been advocating and inculcating (as well as programming and conditioning) the framework of information at the increasing loss and demise of knowledge.

In the last few decades especially there has been an accelerated dumbing down in Western culture that has been noticeable in education as well as in the more recent "wokism" racket alongside the barbaric censorship of free speech and the infantile "cancel culture". This again goes back to my framework of "not-being" as opposed to *beingness*. Sadly, it can now be witnessed that the mode of "not-being" is not only operating throughout technology but increasingly through humans too. Partly to blame is the "cult of personality" syndrome where our societies and cultures compel us more and more to exist solely through the human persona (the "mask") and almost never through the "essence". Cultural institutions and establishments require that a person turns up with a specific type of personality, whether it be corporate, bureaucratic, competitive, devious, logical, and many others. There are some areas where essence has historically been more prominent, such as health care and agriculture, yet even these areas have become more co-opted into the corporatised sector. The cult of personality is an exteriorising mechanism and relates to what I mentioned earlier in this chapter when referring to my notion of the *skin-dweller*. The constant process of living through the personality, and increasingly experiencing life through the exteriorised self, is part of the recombination of the human condition through a subtle means of sociocultural dehumanisation. This is somewhat akin to what philosopher-mystic G. I. Gurdjieff called the "psychopathology of ordinary waking state". In other words, the individual is in a "waking state" during their days despite effectively being still inwardly asleep. And this asleep-while-awake state allows for such abnormality of behaviour and customs to become normalised within the strata of culture.

I propose that as the threshold approaches (a threshold to just where is not yet decided) we shall see increasing signs of abnormality and vulgarity within many of our societies. A random sweep of the media landscape, entertainment industries, and cultural events will no doubt already reveal this (and some indications will be glaring). Yet it is exactly at the point of abnormality and excess where the greatest entry point— or weakness—for the dissolution of the human being can occur. And it is through this entry gate that the apparatuses of technicity (technocracy, transhumanism, and tyranny) will use their advantage to take control. By this time the human being, the individual as well as the collective, will already be emptied out to a certain degree—perhaps just enough to be passively accepting of the new regime of social management. Some commentators have referred to this as the process of *zombiefication* of peoples (see Chapter Eight). Previously, social-psyop operations such as propaganda and mass programming were not referred to publicly by those in positions of political power. It was known about but not mentioned openly. However, that is now changing as world governments are publicly declaring that "enemy" regimes are using psyops (psychological operations) against their peoples, as well as accusing national governments of implementing "false flag" operations. This open display of such terms is unprecedented and may well reflect the times where deep-state actors and meta-governmental bodies have reached a state of arrogance and complacency where such things can be said without public retribution (or even acknowledgement). As an interesting note here, in a January 2023 interview, Nikolai Patrushev who is current secretary of the Security Council of Russia (and was previously the director of the Federal Security Service, the successor to the KGB) made the following statement: "The West has mastered the zombification of people with the help of mass propaganda, and now it seeks to use cognitive weapons, influencing each person on an ad hoc basis using information technology and neuropsychological methods."[8] While not surprising to those people of critical observation it is nonetheless of interest to note that a top intelligence official is accusing a global player of utilising "cognitive weapons" and "neuropsychological methods" to zombify their peoples. And this is surely the case with most modern global regimes, amounting to a form of cognitive warfare against the masses upon an unparalleled scale via propaganda and programming channels. The human condition has long been an object for neuropsychological targeting. It is not an even playing field by any stretch of the imagination. Furthermore, the physical and mental state of the human being has been chosen for deliberate modification—yet, according to what agenda? As I discuss in Chapter Six, it would appear that the sociocultural environment is being terraformed to better acclimatise for a particular mode of life that will affect the modality of the human condition.

We are already seeing the increasing mechanisation of human life through the identification with digital usage and an increasingly automated social life of payments, shopping, and lifestyle choices. Much of communication is now little more than mechanical chatter; unnecessary babble that comes across more as human energy leakage than intelligible conversation. Online life has rapidly deteriorated, and now we see increasing infantilism and irrelevant info-sharing as if in fear of contracting boredom from within the intermittent spaces of silence. The Tower of Babel syndrome may well symbolise the fracturing of our current human civilisation into splintered languages and conversations. We have fast become a confusion of tongues that waggle incessantly, attaching to information and seldom to knowledge. Much is spoken yet little is really said. Modern life for many people is now an environment that lacks any suitable meaning or purpose, and people are opting out of life in droves. As a statistic, in 2022 there were an estimated 1.6 million suicide attempts in the US alone.[9] The suicide rate is highest in "middle-aged white men" according to these statistics. These may be a combination of privileged as well as not so privileged white males. We know from the 2008 financial crash that many once well-to-do bankers committed suicide after their financial world collapsed around them. Would this really be a good enough reason to end one's life? Perhaps what we are seeing here is the lack of real grounding within individuals, a loss of life essence (loss of "soul"), and the fear of losing external dependencies. The persona may appear strong when supported by a powerful exterior environment, yet the inner essence-being is like a child suffering from a life of stunted growth. And increasing reliance upon a technology of "not-being" will only further the stunted growth of the human *being*. The loss of individual purpose and meaning has already become part of the public narrative with Israeli historian Yuval Noah Harari announcing that an automated future brings redundancy to human life and meaning. Harari has stated that the immediate future holds little hope for a new underclass of "irrelevant" and "useless" people. In previous centuries, says Harari, people revolted against exploitation, oppression, tyranny, etc.; now, they fear becoming irrelevant and downgraded: "If we are not careful, we will end up with downgraded humans misusing upgraded computers to wreak havoc on themselves and on the world."[10] Huge numbers of individuals will find themselves living in a society that doesn't need them anymore—or so the prognosis goes. With this in view, it may appear that the destiny of such "will to technology" is one that brings with it a newly arising state of nihilism—*über-nihilism*. Such a form of nihilism speaks of a future that heralds an unknown landscape if the threshold towards technicity is passed. Now it must be asked if humanity is prepared or even willing for this transformation to unfold. The forces of über-nihilism are beckoning.

Notes

1. Arthur Kroker, *Exits to the Posthuman Future* (Cambridge: Polity Press, 2014), 18.

2. See the work of Ian McGilchrist, such as in *The Master and His Emissary* (New Haven, CT: Yale University Press, 2010).

3. See Hannah Arendt's *The Life of the Mind* (New York: Houghton Mifflin Harcourt, 1978).

4. Keith Ansell Pearson, *Viroid Life: Perspectives on Nietzsche and the Transhuman Condition* (London: Routledge, 1997), 124.

5. Keith Ansell Pearson, *Viroid Life: Perspectives on Nietzsche and the Transhuman Condition* (London: Routledge, 1997), 152.

6. The concept of the Fourth Industrial Revolution was introduced through the auspices of the World Economic Forum, and for this reason is highly controversial among many critical thinkers (the author included).

7. See Lewis Mumford's two volumes on *The Myth of the Machine—Technics and Human Development* (1967), and *The Pentagon of Power* (1970).

8. Charlie Nash, "Putin's Potential Successor Exposes the 'Real Power in the West'" in *New Dawn Magazine* (May–June 2023, No.198), 8.

9. https://afsp.org/suicide-statistics/ - last accessed 16 October 2024.

10. Yuval Noah Harari, *21 Lessons for the 21st Century* (London: Jonathan Cape, 2018).

CHAPTER FOUR

Techno-materialism and the forces of über-nihilism

Authority in the middle of the twentieth century has changed its character; it is not overt authority, but anonymous, invisible, alienated authority

—Erich Fromm

The most deadly criticism one could make of modern civilization is that apart from its man-made crises and catastrophes, it is not humanly interesting ...

—Lewis Mumford

As we move along the landscape stretching ahead of us, we begin to see (or to perceive) that there are forces and players that wish to place the entire Earth, and global human civilisation, under the domination of materialism. To be more precise, under the auspices of technicity. These forces of technologically driven materialism (techno-materialism) are initially unfolding within so-called developed and industrialised nations, yet shall no doubt spread further afield. They serve as a prototype for the transformation of human society into a realm of deeply embedded techno-materialism. To execute this process, many high-profile people are sought out (such as politicians, financiers, and celebrities) to be the puppets—the *marionettes*—for promoting this agenda. This is the present state of affairs, regardless of how things may appear upon the spectacle-led surface. As this human-techno mediated threshold approaches, greater forces of chaos will be unleashed at the same time when there is the necessity for a drive towards coherent order. It is this dichotomy of the ordering principle in parallel with chaotic attractors that will usher in the forces pushing for techno programs of control and mediation. An earlier impulse had in fact been introduced into a prior phase of Western modernity around the middle to late nineteenth century that had as its aim the familiarisation with non-physical realms of reality. This was the beginning of the spiritualism movement, alongside early American transcendentalism, theosophy, and occult themes which were to signal the beginning of a metaphysical impulse to prepare human society for a potential change in structures of cognition and consciousness. Before this time, the physical life experience had become mostly one of material content rather than metaphysical exploration. It was coming to a point where it was almost impossible for human culture as a collective to take up the inner developmental impulse. Previously, pursuits of the inner spirit life were a phantasmagorical luxury that few could afford. This situation was dramatically altered by the introduction of spiritualism, seances, after-life phenomena, and eventually the appearance of the "Hidden Masters" (via theosophy) into human affairs. This literally opened the floodgates to a flow of personages that arrived upon the new shores promulgating occult, esoteric, and metaphysical teachings. Yet where there is a notable intervention of such forces, they almost certainly attract their counter-parts of the denying or negating forces of materialism.

As in all previous centuries, many varied social and occult forces were working to keep the transcendental impulse out of human life. This impulse had been replaced by static mystic-religious structures based on rigid protocols rather than inspiration from the inner life. Previous kinetic and dynamic vital impulses that had been introduced into earthly life had by now been corrupted into dogmatic and static systems. And in the years that followed, the forces of deep materialism and techno-driven development significantly accelerated, bringing forward the use of technologies that monitor, track, and regulate human behaviour. Human forms of social management are now rapidly being transferred into artificial structures and arrangements, presided over by machinic, programmed, calculative, and analytic networks. These systems are constantly being referred to as "intelligent" when their mode of cognition and comprehension is code-based programming. Efficient and rational decision making is being labelled as intelligence to the point where humans will soon be mimicking the machines in the false belief that this signifies the new "posthuman" form of intelligence. This indicates why there is now a huge push for the implementation of AI and machinic intellect as this opens the gateway for future developmental potentials to follow the same line. And this line of development will be antithetical to the expansion of genuine human intelligence.

The popularising, and counterfeit, politics of our time are infected with the viral contagion of techno-materialism and the apparatus of control. There is a deep sense of foreboding rising like vapour and spreading like chemical contrails through our still human cultures. It is a mixture of inner disquiet with digitalised existentialism. A decay of materialistic thinking has set in, contributing to the lonely, disconnected age of mass society. Social media platforms stream the cultural wreckage of a modern age with both abstraction and precision. We are witnessing the jetsam and flotsam of social driftwood pollute the waters of cultural materialism. A psychic malaise has been creeping into our societies, providing the script for the psychodrama of our times within the theatre of the absurd. It is the projected trauma of estrangement; a vortex of fragmented energy that accompanies the accelerated machinic impulse within the belly of technicity. Techno-materialism is creating a perfect storm that leaves behind a digital wreckage of data debris. The human psyche-body is in danger of becoming a new hybrid *data-flesh*. The main philosophic "religion" of any post-humanism is entropy, the gradual path to energetic dissolution within an amnesic universe. This is the thinking fuelled by a pseudo-intellectualism coveted by the nerd minds of a tech-utopia materialism. Such a mental view of the world—a fatalism that is flawed by limited perception—calls forth a rationally based nihilism. It is a form of nihilism that keeps us disappointed and expectant at the same time, like a child with a toy it doesn't understand. This polarity confusion of disappointment and expectancy combined with a loss of inner *beingness* creates a new beast—über-nihilism.

The forces of über-nihilism

From the German language, *über* means "over, beyond" and signifies that the new form of nihilism goes beyond or over from the physical and into the metaphysical. A metaphysical nihilism reveals a loss of the inner being, loss of connection between the human being and its organic context. It does not need to be completely negative but rather contextualises the loss of self that occurs when people lose a sense of meaning in life—lose their orientation. This can be most pronounced in the shift between ages—times of transition—as one epoch is dissolving and a new one has yet to fully appear. The nihilism that existed prior to our current times was a rejection of moral and/or religious principles, and a feeling or philosophical perspective that nothing in the world has a real existence or meaning. However, our consensus reality is now being manipulated so the "normal" state of affairs—in a world of deep fakes, post-truth, and narrative manipulation—is that we are not sure if "the world has a real existence" at the best of times. The nihilism that the encroaching era of deep techno-materialism is creating is what I refer to as *über-nihilism*. The spectre of über-nihilism is but the head of a larger creature that represents a broader state of humanity. The historian Oswald Spengler famously announced a century ago that the Western world is ending, and we are witnessing the final season of its civilisational decline. If we are to believe Spengler, then the Western world has been in decline for a solid one hundred years now. And yet, for many people, the world has never seemed more abundant, with access to so much content-rich lifestyles and social satisfiers. Yet, perhaps it is more the case that over the last few decades, just enough of a trickle of meaning and purpose was provided by worldly living so that the spectre of meaninglessness has been kept at bay. Now, however, it would seem that the natives are becoming restless. And not just the natives of the West are becoming restless, but globally. Spengler may have been correct in surmising that the Western world has been in decline for the past century or more; certainly, in our current times, the geo-political Western bloc is fast losing its power base. Yet it seems apparent that something larger is in operation—a planned cross-over to a different evolutionary stream, perhaps? There is certainly an energetic shift apparent across the planet, with increased dissonance, unease, anxiety, trauma, depression, nervousness, and more. Some of these conditions could be put down to a correspondence in the Earth's decreasing magnetic fields and the increasing influx of solar and cosmic radiation. However, a grander psychic imbalance is in play through humanity's collective psychology, and "meta" questions of meaning and purpose are arising.

The English philosopher Colin Wilson believed that modern existentialism—the alienation, nihilism, and boredom of modern life—results from a "fallacy of insignificance". In other words, the feeling that the human being has no worth, and has no role or true place in the world.[1] Further, that such nihilism, related to the human sense of insignificance, is promoted by increased materialism—and specifically what I refer to as techno-materialism. Yet matters have changed dramatically in the world since Wilson produced his prognosis more than fifty years ago. And this has brought us to Yuval Noah Harari's proclamation of the new underclass of "irrelevant" and "useless" people, to which I referred in the previous chapter. Huge numbers of individuals may soon find themselves living in a society that doesn't need them anymore. It is a harder battle to struggle against irrelevance as there is nothing tangible to cling to or to reassure the individual against the encroaching ennui of irrelevance (only the innate sense of self can push against this). This leads to a psychological state of über-nihilism, for such nihilism is ulti- mately a question of truth; a truth about oneself and how a person feels themselves to be within the experience of physical life.

Our external lives are filled with reams of relative truths; from sci- entific, to religious and the philosophic. Modern life has shifted into a maelstrom of varied and diverse subjectivities. Whatever truths were peddled as part of the pre-existing consensus narratives (religion, science, etc.), they are undergoing a vast refurbishment while their replacements do not seem to be arriving any time soon (there is a delay in the "truth supply chain"). Almost every aspect of modern life has become questionable. Scepticism and disbelief (or non-belief) have replaced much of our civilisational questioning. Internal questioning has been substituted with a new form of cultural obedience—internal persuasion from without. When all major global, governmental, and human management systems are founded on untruths and blatant mis- conceptions, then the problem stems from the corrupted core of the sys- tem itself and infuses outwards into the people. Deception is the blood of the current cultural beast. Within such a system, the counterweight to über-nihilism is going to be a form of tyranny and totalitarianism. Any revolution born out of apathy and existential angst will only feed the false kingdom of this world. It has happened before. Tyrannical regimes such as fascism and National Socialism exploited the sense of restless- ness to feed into their own purposes and agenda of authoritarianism. It is because such nihilism produces, or is produced from, an inner dis- quiet that people become unmoored from their grounding, start to drift, and are then much more susceptible to forces of mass formation and false solidarity (as so clearly shown by the work of psychologist Mattias Desmet).[2] Furthermore, this itching sense of disquiet is often covered up through the seeking of activities and distractions that provide a temporary sense of well-being. This is the opportune time for claims of techno-utopia and tech-salvation as a proposed gateway from the rest-lessness and meaninglessness of an empty and/or uncertain existence. According to Seraphim Rose, the spectre of nihilism has already arrived at our shores:

> ... nihilism has become, in our time, so widespread and pervasive, has entered so thoroughly and so deeply into the minds and hearts of all men living today, that there is no longer any "front" on which it may be fought; and those who think they are fighting it are most often using its own weapons, which they in effect turn against themselves.[3]

Über-nihilism is rapidly spreading because there is no longer any relationship—tangible or non-tangible—to even relative truths. The religious, spiritual, cultural, and political ropes of attachment have become irretrievably severed. The only hope that has been offered in the place of the void is technological—a techno-materialism promoted as the machine of ultimate progress. The artificial construct is being praised as the "new authentic". There is no desire or wish for a return to the old systems and structures; nor is there any genuine replacement except for the shiny offerings of technical advancement. And within this void of desperation, people will be almost willing for a new "great reset".

The deepening techno-materialism of the digital age/cage is con-structing a false playground out of the increased dismantling of all the prior structures of morality and meanings. The recent "pandemic" and post-pandemic pressures forced more and more people into online and digital lifestyles. The rising management systems of the carbon-controlled "green economy" will further establish an architecture of monitored and curated needs. This emerging architecture of control is what I have referred to as the "machinic impulse" and it takes the pre-existing forms of nihilism to a new level. Über-nihilism can be viewed as constant uncertainty while untruths are disguised as knowledge when they are nothing more than a power-control structure. This über-nihilism is, I would posit, a loss of meaning and reality-grounding through a new technological world order that strips a person of any sense of inner being and triggers various unseen neuroses. Psycho-analysis tells us that neurosis is part of the humanisation process—the limitation of experience; the fragmentation of perception; the dispossession of internal control. In other words, it is a "falling away from one's being"—a de-centredness—a lack of a moral-spirit centre. This inner void creates disorientation. It is not so much a social-cultural or a political nihilism but a psychological one. It is a denial and (dis)belief centred upon the same thing—a nothingness or zero-space. Out of this zero-space may arise a techno-mediated "world of the absurd"—a machinic rationality that becomes the new irrational form of narrative. This new "irrational narrative" would have the aim of becoming the next form of world structure. However, it is necessary first to dismantle the old narratives that held the prior order together. In terms of a power structure, it would be better to crush the old narratives so that their remnants do not try to rise up to confront the new programming. This was seen with the National Socialism of the Nazis: it wasn't only a physical new order but also, importantly, a psychological one. The new order must dethrone its imagined enemies to declare a new security state, or world order of security.

A new form of social organisation is coming into existence that represents this über-nihilistic era (or the dying cultural age). It represents a kind of lucid absurdity where technique and precision are paramount, and displays an appalling insensitivity towards the human and the "being" of humanity. This über-nihilist form of organisation corresponds to a terraforming and transformation of the Earth and society by machines, artificial intellects, and the inhuman ideology of social management and engineering that accompanies it. Its aim is to become a highly centralised power regime that consumes all forms of knowledge and truth divergent to its own ideological narratives: "For if there is no truth, power knows no limit save that imposed by the medium in which it functions, or by a stronger power opposed to it."[4] The ideological narrative, from the über-nihilist power structure's point of view, will be one of perfect rationality and technological progress that provides for a world of total "liberation". Yet it shall be a techno-materialist's pseudo-utopia as, in truth, it will be the vastest, and most efficient, digital iron cage humans have ever known—for it will be pervasive and untouchable. Yet this is not the most worrying issue. The more disturbing aspect here is that there is a power-drive to establish the organisation for a "new earth" that resists the natural, cyclic evolutionary impulses.

The core object of this project—the *technicity project*—is for a transformation of humankind into a new planetary species body. It shall be a planetary species greatly reduced in number and highly segregated by status and servitude. And most importantly, it will be based on a collective humanised mass that function at a lower vibration of being and self. And a small number of wealthy and powerful individuals, with immense hubris, are attempting to manage and steer this transition to favour their materialistic goals at the expense of the many.

The philosopher Friedrich Nietzsche, who perhaps recognised this condition better than most, said that under certain circumstances, "Nihilism might be the sign of a process of incisive and most essential growth, and of mankind's transit into completely new conditions of existence."[5] This is because the human being—the new mutation—is rootless, discontinuous with a past that is being dismantled and destroyed, and is eager for the new apocalypse (i.e., "revelation") to emerge in its place. And yet, there are simultaneously materialistic forces pushing to create the mass-minded collective as opposed to individualised people. The "new human" of the devolutionary techno-materialist path will be a reduced version of themselves—the *robosapiens* that is the profane human being. Before human civilisation arrives at that threshold (what some have termed as the "bifurcation"), there is the increasing danger of a rising incoherence that paralyses people between the extremes of external power and an increasing internal powerlessness. This encroaching "lucid absurdity" is like the emperor's new clothes where very few people are recognising the blatant incongruity of our mainstream narratives; hence, there is almost no one around to ask the question as to how we can transcend the perceptual limits of the world. It would seem that a certain form of inner truth and sincerity is required for such an enterprise.

Such a time of über-nihilism—a form of ideological and spiritual purposelessness—is when things fall apart because they no longer have any centre to hold them together. And yet, a form of numbed daily life continues. The external events of any age are a projection of humanity's inner state and psyche; only that, at certain times this collective condition becomes more visible upon the world stage. During the phases of transition, or redirection, there are fewer commonly accepted points of orientation, and the compass no longer has a magnetic north. In times of changing magnetics (metaphorically speaking), people are more willing to adopt the "obedience to security" as an easy external dependency. And yet, (über)nihilism, insecurity, meaningless-ness, and lack of purpose, are not the cause but the symptoms. The ori-entation of the individual is an internal question rather than an external one. The individual has to come to their own sense of coherence. In the words of Václav Havel: "The principles of control and discipline ought to be abandoned in favour of self-control and self-discipline."[6] The individual's sense of self has to come to the fore, otherwise the indi-vidual can find themselves lost to the energetic forces of massification and external manipulation that are the programs for the current techno-materialist agenda. Within this agenda, the digital shadows replicate the shadows of the real world. The digital bodies cast their electronic shadows as physical replicas, and the human presence is placed in exile.

As I have previously mentioned, the human act of attention—to come into attendance with the world—is getting stepped back and replaced with a digital presence and a replicated attendance. The shad-ows cast by über-nihilism become a digital shade for obscuring hid-den human traumas. No wonder then that there is such an energy of nihilism lurking within the human psyche, as the sterility of techno-materialism, cultural vulgarity, and widespread psychological malaise disturbs the collective field. An artificial construct is attempting to push in, to barge its way onto the Earth, yet it is no real substitute for the membrane of organic life. And yet, organic life is being sliced open through the slick scalpel of technology and we are being neuro-invaded with the debris and wreckage of information, data, and digital dirge that fills the aetheric seas. The externalised mind is under siege, and it is a dangerous place to be afloat without proper mooring or anchor. The psychic playground has been taken over by a cacophony of insurgents that are attempting to colonise our resonant, inner spaces with a fre-quency that works to lower its current vibratory rate.

It is little wonder that the über-nihilist feels adrift from any meta-physical meaning or contact, existing in an almost constant state of suspicion; not only against incumbent institutions and fixed systems, but especially against the invisible trackers and surveillant apparatuses that codify how we move through the techno-materialist world. Sensors attach themselves to our words, our deeds, and soon to our thoughts—pre-empting our every move. Our lies and truths lived through, day and night, under sensors and censorship; suffering from the new disorder of "data-insomnia" for there is no sleep within the realm of data. The silent machinery of mass surveillance never sleeps for it never trusts us, the citizens, and is forever suspicious of our uprising, of a hostile insurgency from the carbon-bodied inhabitants. The techno-materialist colonisation project is morphing into what French philosopher and cultural theorist Paul Virilio describes as "endo-colonization" which happens when authority-driven societies turn against and colonise their own people. In other words, it is an internal colonisation by a state over its own population, especially by taking control over their bodies or biological integrity. On the microsocial level, the human body increasingly becomes a target site for technology itself. Endo-colonisation is an emptying out of the old patterns and organisation and a recalibration (or re-territorialisation) through techno imperatives that disrupts the human and social balance. Increasingly powerful and pervasive technologies attempt to secure, manage and organise human behaviour. Techno-materialism works to de-territorialise, de-contextualise, and de-historicise the human trajectory. If this doesn't trigger a rise of über-nihilism, nothing will.

In the philosophy of existentialism, people create their own meaning throughout their lives and through the choices they make. In absurdism, instead of trying to create meaning, or false meaning, people stare into the face of meaninglessness and may choose to rebel against it and enjoy life through this constant rebelliousness. In regular nihilism, there appears to be no objective meaning to life. In über-nihilism, under the auspices of techno-materialism, the individual observes the artificial construct arising around them and thinks of the metaphysical void where the sacred is substituted for the unseen (yet metallic tasting) organisational threads of management and control. It is unsettling to say the least.

Notes

1. Colin Wilson, *The Age of Defeat* (London: Aristeia Press, 2018).
2. See Mattias Desmet's *The Psychology of Totalitarianism* (White River Junction, VT: Chelsea Green Publishing Co, 2022).
3. Seraphim Rose, *Nihilism: The Root of the Revolution of the Modern Age* (Platina, CA: St. Herman of Alaska Brotherhood, 1994/2018), 11.
4. Seraphim Rose, *Nihilism: The Root of the Revolution of the Modern Age* (Platina, CA: St. Herman of Alaska Brotherhood, 1994/2018), 79.
5. Cited in Seraphim Rose, *Nihilism: The Root of the Revolution of the Modern Age* (Platina, CA: St. Herman of Alaska Brotherhood, 1994/2018), 91.
6. Vaclav Havel, *The Power of the Powerless: Citizens Against the State in Central Eastern Europe* (London: Routledge, 1985), 77.

CHAPTER FIVE

The metaphysical heretics of Lesser Reality

Those who are able to see beyond the shadows and lies of their culture will never be understood, let alone believed, by the masses

—Plato

Metaphysics is not so much about that which is "beyond" physics as this suggests that what is metaphysical lies only in the beyond zone and not within. The metaphysical fire, which signifies the Origin, Source, Absolute, or Intelligence of all existence, is behind time, space, causation, and manifestation, as well as being integrated as all those aspects. The metaphysical fire is as much *beyond* as it is *within*, for there is never a state that is void of it—even the void itself is an expression of the metaphysical fire. In Cabbalistic terms, there are four levels of reality, or emanations: divine, spiritual, psychological, and physical. The divine corresponds to the Source of All; the spiritual is non-being, or what modern science refers to as the quantum vacuum, zero-point field, the implicate order, or the void. The psychological is the first manifestation or being; again, what science would call the cosmic background radiation or cosmic energy. And the physical is the world of matter, organisms, and of material sense. These are gradations of existence, with all higher emanations integrated or forming a part of all lower gradations. In other words, the physical realm of matter contains the psychological, the spiritual, and the divine—only that they are hidden to plain view (perception). What this means is that the metaphysical impulse (or Fire/Light/Absolute) is existent—*hidden within*—all states of existence, including our material realm. And this, for much of human history, has been a grand heresy.

It is not necessary here to go through a historical stocktake of heresies (the list would be very long!), yet even a passing glance would pick up Gnostic trails (including Catharism, Manichaeism), mystical and occult streams, and almost anything that tackles the dogmatic control structures of orthodoxy. Heresy has been an easy and cheap strategy to attack and dismantle perceived threats against dominant narratives. Heresy has been the label that stigmatises those people, thinking, beliefs, ideologies, and movements, etc., that defy or go against the ruling narratives and control apparatus of the time. Heresies also help to point out to those with critical awareness that they live under a form of totalitarianism, in some degree or other. Such sociocultural control apparatuses seek to indoctrinate the populace within their domain into accepting particular thinking patterns. These patterns, naturally, are established to reinforce and support the incumbent power structures. The concept of heresy is brought out and utilised as a means of involving people—the "public"—within the controlling system. In an age of secularisation, the controlling narrative has shifted from a top-down religious power structure into a technologically enforced "cage of modernity". This is akin to sociologist Max Weber's notion of the "Iron Cage"; or more recently, to writer Philip K. Dick's vision of the "Black Iron Prison". The new secular techno-materialism is bringing about technocratic governance as a dominating narrative, and its affiliated religion of transhumanism is providing for the next priestly class of tech-elites and billionaires. Together they establish what will strive to become the governing apparatus of technocracy—the modern totalitarian system masquerading as the new mode of twenty-first-century global authority. And the notion of heresy has been modified from quasi-religious sectarian cults into the modern conspiracy.

The modern-day heretic is now the much-derided conspiracy theorist, or anyone who dares to defy the consensus narratives. From time immemorial the dominant control apparatus has sought to centralise its power, and this means it must denounce any recognition of direct access to knowledge (which it views as power). Also, the external apparatus of the hierarchical control system cannot be reflected in a metaphysical system. For this reason, the Christian Church did not wish for a "hierarchy of angels" to become recognised, although we have people such as Pseudo-Dionysius the Areopagite and Thomas Aquinas to thank for bringing these systems into human cognition and awareness. Material power structures do not care for metaphysical realities to come out of hiding. This is why such perspectives are branded as heretical and their proponents persecuted into silence or put to death.

A metaphysical perspective is one that recognises how all existence is integrated and unified, and that what lies without also lies within for there is no exterior, only internal degrees or gradations of perceptual experience (existence). The phenomenal universe which we observe and participate within is a Lesser Reality—a reflection or gradation from the Greater Reality. It is within this Lesser Reality that our current "Game of Life" is playing out. A modern heresy is that of the simulation hypothesis which states that human existence is not in fact "real" but being played out within a simulated structure or game. This is an update of the Gnostic perspective that humanity is living within a reality created not by Source/Creator but by a demiurge (a "lesser god"), and in this sense it is somewhat a flawed and thus false reality. Whether we are avatars or amnesiac souls within material bodies, the playground is relatively the same. What the simulation hypothesis does is merely to update the scenario based on modern vocabulary and context. The Gnostics didn't have computers in their day (and hence the computer vocabulary); likewise, the modern tech-gnostics don't wish to speculate within the Christian or any other religious-spiritual theology and vocabulary.

The overarching situation is one whereby seekers of each age are attempting to penetrate into the nature of the human condition vis-à-vis its correspondence with the true nature of reality. Modern terminology is now required so as to pinpoint the attention and focus of the modern-orientated individual. You don't need to be religious to accept the Greater Reality. The Absolute is not a bearded bloke or a jealous deity of judgement. Belief is not necessary when it comes to approaching reality for belief is merely an early stage upon the path of realisation. You only need an urge to wonder; an inner pull (or magnetic centre) to know, and the will to seek. The metaphysical fire wishes to be known—and you only need to want to know it too. If we can speak of anything, we can call it a law of resonance. The knower and the known must frequent the same frequency for there to be a correspondence. This is the "field" where the meeting has to take place—a "field" of frequency as well as a zone of correspondence. As the Persian mystic-poet Jalāl al-Dīn Rumi wrote:

> Out beyond ideas of wrongdoing and rightdoing,
> there is a field. I'll meet you there.
> When the soul lies down in that grass,
> the world is too full to talk about.
> Ideas, language, even the phrase "each other"
> doesn't make any sense.
> The breeze at dawn has secrets to tell you.
> Don't go back to sleep.
> You must ask for what you really want.
> Don't go back to sleep.
> People are going back and forth across the doorsill
> where the two worlds touch.
> The door is round and open.
> Don't go back to sleep.[1]

This field exists beyond our localised ideas and morality codes. The physical, sensory world is too full of the lower vibrations—"too full to talk about"—and this can block the perceptive senses. The ideas and language of the material realm have no meaning within the "frequency field" that provides "the doorsill where the two worlds touch". Yet the seeker must resist being pulled back into the denser senses and lower frequency of the physical realm—"Don't go back to sleep." Rumi, and many others like him, clothed themselves within the robes of their time, be it Islam, Sufism, or any other sociocultural-religious context that was necessary to operate within. The metaphysical impulse knows how to roam unimpeded by the contexts and circumstances of the time. Its core frequency is not of this realm, yet it acts through operations— "manifestations"—that are of the physical domain. Religious and spiritual vehicles have been utilised as carriers for these manifestations, yet they are certainly not the only means. It also depends upon what the main mediums or carriers are at the time within the specific culture (whether religions, legends, myths, tales, etc.). These are often appropriated for maximum dispersal; yet many more mediums, largely unsuspected, are simultaneously utilised for this purpose. The "heretics" are the visible ones; the grand heresy remains hidden within and operates largely without hindrance. And the "grand heresy" of the *metaphysical fire* still rages in our times. Unfortunately, most people remain oblivious to this. They have fallen asleep among the meadows of attractive flowers and amid the scents that tempt the senses. However, an odd and troublesome wind is now blowing through those meadows and disturbing peoples' sleep.

The flowery meadows are not so cosy anymore as an ill wind is stirring those who slumber and arousing people through discomfort and disarray. Uncertainty looms everywhere; the façades of normalcy are slipping down, and the trusted institutions of this reality are showing their false masks. The metaphysical fire is beginning to burn away the outer paintwork, showing the rotten wood underneath. The gatekeepers of stolen power are attempting to cover up the sun by spraying their chemical clouds; yet still, the metaphysical fire comes through. And it is becoming fiery now. It is coming close to another round of its cycle. Flares, outbursts, and eruptions will soon be blasting towards our physical sphere as we cling to its surface like a receiving-transmitting membrane. And it shall all be a matter of frequency. As the great inventor and receiver Nikola Tesla said, if you want to find the secrets of the universe, think in terms of energy, frequency, and vibration. Any vibrational frequency can create as well as destroy, depending upon the corresponding frequency of the receiver. As the metaphysical fire comes to light (and to alight on) our domain, we shall have the fire to guide us or to burn us. No hazmat suits will protect the unprepared. It shall all be a question of perception. Is the heresy a greater truth—or do the dominant consensus narratives speak the truth to us? As above, so below—all is in correspondence. Hiding within the shadowy rock of Plato's cave will not shield anyone from the penetrating fire. It is only the metaphysical fire that does not burn. Instead, it fills the cells of the body with a heightened, finer energy and renews the human vessel. The time is approaching where we shall need to march forward and go forth upon a new path. We can choose to stay within the rocky, shadowy cave; or we can walk lighter upon the sunlit path.

No amount of machinery will lighten the human vessel—it will only serve to automate it further and close down its receptors. Like any fuel cell, it will eventually wind down to a stop if it cannot be recharged. The devolutionary path is strewn full of those objects that came to their final stop when the fuel cell ran dry. It was, and remains, a closed pathway.

You only get so far, despite the shiny promises offered at the beginning. As circumstances become increasingly polarised, the choices of fear or revelation shall become ever more visible. The dark cave is the refuge of the fearful. The sunlit path is the abode for the revellers of the revealed. Within the dark cave, synthetic narratives are deliberately created and spread with intent. These synthetic narratives are a falsehood, a mirage of illusions, that deal in the manipulation of materialised events. This inverted kaleidoscope reveals nothing for it is based itself on nothingness. Yet the dark cave view does not know, cannot conceive or be made aware, that there is no "nothingness"—there is only *every-thingness*. There is no empty void as there is no vacuum, no so-called "space". There is only energy, frequency, and vibration. Everywhere. The only void that exists is in our beliefs and the illusion that maintains them. The void is our sense of separation from this *everythingness* of energy. And yet we have a constant feeling that we carry around with us, a lingering niggle or a faint residue of memory, that gives us the sense that we are missing something. There is a gap in this reality of ours, and yet we miss this, so enthralled we are with playing our roles—of being within *The Game*. The subjective world is a fiction; it is a "reality game" with set roles to play and where the script is constantly being rewritten. This drama of the artificial, synthetic narrative will become the new void where our very consciousness is a dream within the dream of the artificial sleep.

Life within the Lesser Reality is an open playing field that does not need to be dangerous by itself. It only becomes so through what we put into it through our thought forms, desires, and obsessions. It is our subjective beliefs, ideals, opinions, convictions, greed, and all else that make the playing field hazardous. Reality is a canvas that we paint our visions, illusions, or our delusions upon. The realm of Lesser Reality is an amalgam, an accumulation and fusion, of all our thinking and projected dreams, wishes, ideals, etc. It is a realm that is populated by those aspects—elemental beings or egregores?—that have sprung from the projections put forth from human minds. People have martyred themselves for the sake of their beliefs, their sense of truth, their morals or values, yet not for the sake of reality itself. This Lesser Reality, being a result of our own psychic imbalance, can absorb everything, sucking everything into itself. It also allows for all possibilities and potentialities. Chaos and order abound—but not in absolute terms. Our playground has become a form of negated reality that reflects as well as inverts.

It is like an ocean: it can seem polluted or crystal clear, depending on whether the mind that perceives it is cluttered or cleansed. When the receiver has been cleansed, the reflection of what is beyond appears in it. And here, in this shared reality of humankind, fantasies and delusions occupy people's minds and prevent them from working properly. And this makes the realm of negated reality appear unstable, unpredictable, and sometimes frightening. Yet it's not this negated or inverted reality that frightens people: what frightens people is the unknowing, and the sense that perhaps they got it all wrong. And everything they thought, or loved, or put their investment of time and energy into, may not be what they thought it was, or may not be that important or even helpful to them. And then that niggling sense of missing something comes back. And they know that they are out of time, and that they may have to return and repeat the whole game all over again until they start to realise it for what it is.

No one likes to admit that they have been deceived. Worse still, that they got it all wrong and now perhaps they'll need to change how they see things—how they think, believe, and maybe even how they live. No one wishes to learn that they have based their life on a lie, on an illusion. Nietzsche got it right when he noted that when you gaze long into the abyss, the abyss gazes also into you. This abyss is the *everything-ness* upon which Lesser Reality is constructed. It can neither be created nor destroyed. It is only our belief models of reality that get destroyed or deconstructed and reassembled. And it can only undergo this dismantling when the perceiver places the inner being as central to their existence. Truths can be sought but not gained until first the lies and self-deceptions can be recognised and put aside. Perceptive limitations must first be recognised otherwise one is not able to go beyond them. The present game of negated reality begins with amnesia—a veil of oblivion—that is wrapped over our senses. And we have until the end of the game to awaken—to remember. Everything begins with a mystery that very quickly gets turned into normalcy; the everyday; the humdrum tap-tap-tap of our lives. We don't know where we're going and yet we fail to see the beauty of the mystique in this. We fail to be enchanted by the miracle of the everyday because it soon gets locked into a set groove that then becomes the predictable channel of our lives. This consistent groove, like a song track on repeat, keeps people away from prying too far over the top of their reality boxes. There are plenty of false pathways to lead a person down a rabbit hole. And yet, all mainstream narratives need to be questioned. The strappings of the phenomenal world are like a straitjacket over our senses. And when they are stripped away, what is left?

The Lesser Reality perpetuates itself by getting everyone to use the same tools created by the illusions of that reality. Everything to a fish will resemble life within the fishbowl. Reality cannot be seen directly for what it is unless a person can first step away from it. When we look out at the world, at reality, we are looking into a mirror. After all, meanings are derived from the context of our world, our perceived reality. Perhaps because we have no definitive answers in this world, we create ideologies and belief systems to explain a realm beyond our present reality. Humanity exists within a deep ignorance that only deepens the further it dives into materialism, like diving deeper in the depths of the Mariana Trench. Unfathomable mysteries exist because of our deep ignorance of the world in which we live. Why is there ignorance? Because of the amnesia we carry with us into this incarnation. Why do we arrive with such amnesia? Because that is the nature of the game. We have to figure out the game by firstly not knowing about it. We do this by first trying to figure ourselves out. Then we begin to understand what the playing field of the game is all about and what we can do— or need to do—while we are here. Yet this "awakening", as it is often termed, is not easy; not easy at all. Why? Because there are too many dreamlike revelries that fill our waking minds. This also is the nature of the game. Lesser Reality is a responsive, inclusive realm. It is like a living, intelligent gel that conforms to our shapes. Not so much physical shapes but according to the shapes of our thoughts, emotions, and mental projections.

Our sense of reality is a continual revelation as it reveals itself to us according to *how we are*. The more we are revealed to ourselves, the more of this reality is likewise revealed to us. It is a science. And the only true science is metaphysical. That which is loosely called science, where people prod and poke the matter-energy substrate, is like a child in the sandpit playing with, or throwing around, their toys. Scientists cry too, just as much as the child in the sandpit. Tears of frustration; sometimes of joy and wonder. Yet this science is engaging with a Lesser Reality, a substratum within which we dwell. We can only make assumptions and speculations about the world. With each step there needs to be a modicum of observant awareness, for we are not stepping upon known ground but the pebbles of uncertainty. This world creates revelations through daydreams, and possibilities through the unknown. Living within the Lesser Reality, without awareness, an individual becomes an automaton, not dissimilar from a machine. Bodies are guided, operating upon minimal cognition. The individual responds to a labyrinth of stimuli as a robotic sensory apparatus. They are receiving yet interpreting little as through a darkened conditioned lens. Perception is as if peering through a slither in the veil.

Human consciousness is both a reflection of this negated reality as well as an imprint back into it; in this manner, the perception trap sustains itself. Each species has a different type of brain which interprets the world—its environment—differently. The human perception of the world is not reality itself but rather the brain's representation of reality. Human perception is therefore a roadmap of reality but is not reality itself. It can be said to be a simulation of reality—and humans live within their own specific images. Reality gets reproduced through each individual and distinct receiver of it. It is not apprehended *as it is* but through a representation of it. We live within the reflections of reality, gazing indistinctly. People live within their heads more than they realise (and the external power structures know this). Our senses inform us of reality based on specific interpretations of the raw data. Mess with the interpreting process and a different reality ensues. Our inverted reality has come into being because synthetic narratives have created worldviews for us that skew our vision and thus our understanding. We have been programmed into *seeing* a particular version of the world, which is upside-down so that it can incorporate the twisted elements that maintain humanity largely within its own asylum of cognitive limitations. Perhaps our great flaw is that we are not able to grasp reality because we are the ones participating in its creation. And humans go around and around chasing their tails trying to fathom the deep mystery of an "objective reality" not understanding that they are swimming within its very waters. Humans are unable to fully perceive or comprehend the nature of their existence because they have largely misrepresented their relationship to reality. Or rather, the programming within this realm has presented a misrepresentation to humans which we have thus far been unable to break from. Our deep longing is this silent inner knowing of how we have created this fundamental separation. And yet, the more we ignore this, the more we become the ghosts. We humanise this separation and make it into the "suffering of existence" as if this phantasmagorical pain is part of the side effects of having a physical life.

Humanity creates its own monsters as well as its angels. The story gets entangled through our ongoing fantasies, and we expect each person who joins the club to step into the same story. There are even those few groupings of "game bullies" who are trying to push their rules of the game onto everyone else, as we can now witness through the rush to techno-materialism. Metaphysical aspects are increasingly being denied in this reality as they pose a threat. And yet, ironically, it is the very people who deny metaphysics who pose a risk to their own sanity. Those who live in denial of a metaphysical reality often consider it a danger, for they dislike the unknown and prefer to cling to the driftwood of illusory certainty. Without knowing it, such people may subconsciously fear the loss of illusion. They rally for the continuation of false certainty at all costs—and this is where the machinic impulse has got a power over them. The machinic impulse is a power-control structure that knowingly manipulates the Lesser Reality and thus the game. This power-control structure (aka the machine) can be said to have been established and operated by a collective or soul-group; a family of "hidden hands". It is the nature of the machine to distort Lesser Reality. There are programs of the machine too that attempt to create negative connotations of the Lesser Reality experience. We should beware of the negating programs of the machine that aim to cultivate fear, anxiety, and anger within the participants of Lesser Reality. Be aware of those materialistic skeletons that masquerade as silicon prophets.

Life can be indistinct, abstract, absurd even. It can seemingly lack meaning, yet this is only a projection from one's own subjective world. If a person encounters meaninglessness, then they have removed themselves from an evolutionary frequency and de-synched into a splintered vibration. There is no vacuum in existence—it simply does not and cannot exist. A vacuum is a myth, a scientific falsity. A barren reality is the projection from a barren mind. It is a mind that vibrates at a machinic frequency. There are those people who seek for a "barren reality" for they pursue a nihilistic path. It is their program. Many such programs exist (and are supplied) as software for creating an experiential terrain decoupled from a harmonic resonance. Such programs may also cultivate the conditioned desire for a state of not-being—that is, a revolt against existence. And some people are just born (incarnated) to be natural saboteurs within the game. The machine operates to prevent a true understanding of the nature of reality. It also seeks to keep people asleep within the game and unaware of the nature of their cognitive containment field.

Many people live life as if it were a dream. Yet few live it as a lucid dream. We seldom think about managing reality as we've been conditioned to accept that reality manages us. This is a passive perception of reality, not an active one. There are too many people who go through life as if they are in mourning or grief. A constant sadness, hopelessness, depression, apathy, and a general lack of interest in the world around them. On the other side of this are those people who seem to live in a constant state of "emotional emergency", where every small thing triggers a heightened emotional response. There are too many contaminants within this inverted realm of Lesser Reality. There are many and varied contagions, affecting minds, hearts, and bodies. And there is a distinct lack of inner will to counter these intrusions and vital energy infections. The aim of the machine is to create a spiritual abyss where people seeking their connection to Source will be returned with an empty black hole. But this is because the black hole will be in the exterior, and not the interior. And the fault lies in looking without for what has always existed within, and through the within back into the Source of All. Life inside the machine is but a dream. Humanity has arrived at a new stage upon its path and the threshold ahead beckons. There is no time now to mourn the loss of an old reality for a new perceptive reality awaits. Illusions may move us, but they should not become an inner driving force. Our illusions within the game only exist as a provisional stage during this crossing of the threshold. The temporary malaise of the physical world can be utilised as a trigger to push humankind beyond the threshold. If we remain too long within this final decaying of an old cycle, then we will be ushered into a world-building phase of a "techno-terraformed" world.

Note

1. Coleman Barks & John Moyne (Trans.), *The Essential Rumi* (New York: Harper, 1995), 36.

CHAPTER SIX

World-building and techno-terraforming

We must learn to recognize what is working in the world and respond accordingly for the sake of the world

—Rudolf Steiner

As human civilisation passes further into a materialised existence, particular forces shall arise that find a material domain to be a preferred environment. Each epoch of civilisation contends with forces, known and unknown, according to humanity's state of development, awareness, and in correspondence to the form of existing cultures and societal structures. Forces that impinge and participate within human life in this realm do so relative to the time and place. In other words, it can be said that forces involved within the evolutionary journey of humanity are consistently adapting according to the epoch. Human life upon this planet is now transitioning into an era of techne (*technē*). In its original sense, in Greek philosophy, this term signified the mechanical arts; and Aristotle viewed techne as representing the imperfection of the human imitation of nature. That is, the mechanical arts were imperfect in attempting to imitate, reproduce, and/or substitute the processes of nature. The mechanical arts also represented not only the mechanical objects/structures themselves but also the sets of ordered practices and skills that went along with them. Techne is not only, in modern terms, a piece of technology, but also the behaviour, lifestyle practices, attitudes, skill sets, and more, than run alongside, or are instigated, by technology in order for its inclusion into human life. If human behaviour becomes more automated by a piece of technology, such as the use of a spell-checker (as is being used here), then the laziness in personal grammar that results from this is also a part of the techne of the computer and word processing software. What this suggests is that the direction that humanity is taking, in the name of progress, is towards establishing a new environmental infrastructure that will reorganise and recalibrate human behaviour. It will also require a readaptation as this is not a minor transition, such as a generational linear progression, but a major transformation in how life is experienced upon the planet. Human adaptation also requires an adaptation in consciousness.

Each aeon, or major period of history, brings with it a particular mode of consciousness. For example, the Swiss philosopher Jean Gebser noted how human consciousness is not continuous but is in transition; and that these transitions, or switching of modes, are not continuous but rather "mutations". They undergo a leap, or jump—sometimes a radical switching—that is not linear. Gebser outlined the following con-sciousness structures: i) the archaic; ii) the magical; iii) the mythical; iv) the mental; and v) the integral. Each of these structures framed how people perceived the world around them and the forces within it. Such consciousness structures also influenced how particular worldviews, behaviours, and environments emerged. At each stage, *how* we think affects what we create (as explained in Chapter Five). Also, the nature of a culture or civilisation is in correspondence to the way in which its dominant consensus reality is defined. A form of inverted reality, as discussed previously, no doubt causes ruptures or splintering within the human psyche. According to Gebser, humanity has now entered the "integral structure" phase that is pushing through from the pre-vious epoch of the mental structure, and this is now being projected into how our cultures and civilisations are being reconstructed. The world-building of each aeon of history is influenced by the incumbent structure of human consciousness (which is itself influenced by cosmic factors).[1] According to Gebser, the integral consciousness structure was made evident by a new relationship to space and time. In some ways, we can see how this is manifesting through our increasingly digitalised cultures that have drastically altered how people experience space-time relations. Consciousness, and intelligence, are themselves unseen, and often unrecognised, forces that have huge influence upon human life. Equally, how an environment is built up also then reflects back certain influences and impacts upon a person's consciousness.

A very basic analogy here is the difference between being immersed in nature, in a natural environment, as opposed to being immersed within a high-density urban environment. In this context, the human being in cultures across the globe is increasingly being exposed not only to a digitised ecosystem but also to an unprecedented electromagnetic one. We are literally existing within a sea of unseen, and hidden, forces. It can be said that the planet Earth is currently undergoing a mode of *terraforming* (literally meaning "earth-shaping"). Terraforming is the process of deliberately modifying the ecology (atmosphere, temperature, etc.) of a planet, or similar body, to make it habitable for humans to live on. And from all indications, the current "form" that is under construction will be amenable to a certain type of intelligence. For starters, it will be kind to an intelligence that understands how to use digital tools, apps, and software. And it will be unkind to those intelligences that find it difficult to get their heads around all this "digital, online stuff". It will be kind to those who are willing to accept a life within the grid of digital-everything—finances, surveillance, internet-of-bodies, 5G/6G/7G/8G, etc.—and it will be unkind to those wishing to escape from 24/7 surveillance and wishing for a less digitally dense lifestyle.

Any sufficiently advanced species visiting this planet could be forgiven for thinking that a terraforming project is underway for adapting the planet Earth for a machinic intelligence or AI form of species. We only have to look at the highly dense electromagnetic environment, the masts and antennas, the cameras and surveillance systems, the monitoring satellites, etc., to see this. In 1987 the English poet Heathcote Williams published his epic poem "Autogeddon" about the impact of the automobile. In it he wrote:

> If an alien was to hover a few hundred yards above the planet
> It could be forgiven for thinking
> That cars were the dominant life-form,
> And that human beings were a kind of ambulatory fuel cell:
> Injected when the car wished to move off,
> And ejected when they were spent.[2]

The same can be said for the world of today if we replace "car" with "technological infrastructure". Only that the object of containment has changed; it is no longer the car but the digital ecosystem, yet the subject of the containment (i.e., us) has remained the same. If humanity is to transform itself from being "a kind of ambulatory fuel cell" within the megamachine, then we need a recalibration of what technology means for human life.

For some, what is being described here is the shift into transhumanism, alongside the rise of a civilisational technocracy. What is also being described is a new mode of a physical environment—technomaterialism—that does not need to rely on physical solidity for it to be material. The new solidification of the world is through immersion into the physical-digital ecosystem—the new ethereal mode of matter-reality. I have referred to this previously as the "material fallacy" that represents a re-territorialising of physical matter.[3] This fallacy is that the continuing encapsulation of the human being into artificial constructs (such as digital environments) is a deepening deception of materiality. And such an environment also affects the cognitive functioning of the mind as it becomes ever more deeply immersed into an electrified realm. This will designate the new domain of techne where different cognitive skills will be necessary. It will also frame how humanity is tracked, monitored, catalogued, and processed. Humanity will become symbiotic. New processes of integration are being established between the biological world, the digital, and the electronic. What may be emerging here is a wholly different planetary formation that merges genes, machines, and societies. The human intelligence that will result from this is, as yet, unformed and, in most ways, unknown. And it may become home to more than one form of intelligence. This is the pivotal crisis for humanity as it approaches the threshold of a transmutation; and there are powerful forces pushing for the transition to shift into techno-materialism. As I have mentioned previously, there is the danger that as people slip further into an ecosystem of automation, not only their behaviour but also their state of cognition will be affected. The unconscious human may, by degrees, be transformed into the *robosapiens* where behaviour patterns and cognitive perception are limited to a very low level. Such a person will, effectively, be little more than a cog in the machine. And the machine will be well oiled by AI-regulated infrastructures. Yet the real "hidden force" in such an electrified world may be something more nefarious than the automated human being.

The ongoing terraforming of the natural, organic world opens itself up for a replacement by a "machinic civilisation" based on technocratic governance and processes of techne. When the ecosystems of nature are broken down, reduced to material systems, then the building blocks for artificial structures—structures devoid of organic life—are established which "host" the manifestation and expression of anti-developmental forces (or what I sometimes refer to as *entropic forces*). The present times are hyper-materialistic and heavily intellect dominant. This allows for an organisation of human thinking where free speech, human imagination, and intuition are highly controlled and subjected to monitoring, management, and technocratic administration. If this continues then it is likely to lead to a state whereby the human species, unknowing to itself, will have lost the ability for true, genuine thinking. The inner world will have become diminished, and any inner, developmental impulses become overridden by material forces. Furthermore, we may be oblivious to the many unseen fields that make up our ecosystem of electro-energies. These energies are sub-nature. They are part of living existence—as all existence is vibration and frequency—yet they represent a lower form of life vibration. According to Austrian mystic-philosopher Rudolf Steiner, electricity is a form or state of light in a *sub-material* state. That is, it is a form of light that is lower in frequency than the level of natural light—such as we find from our sun or the biophoton light from our biological cells—and so this lower vibrational form of "artificial light" is what Steiner termed as "sub-nature". It is because of this that Steiner warned humankind to be cautious not to build cultures dependent or based on electricity. An electro-ecosystem will only serve to draw us further away from our natural environments and into a lower vibrational state of sub-nature. In a lecture from 1925, Steiner says:

> There are very few as yet who even feel the greatness of the spiritual tasks approaching man in this direction. Electricity, for instance, celebrated since its discovery as the very soul of Nature's existence, must be recognised in its true character—in its peculiar power of leading down from Nature to Sub Nature. Only man himself must beware lest he slide downward with it.[4]

Rudolf Steiner made great efforts to outline aspects of the various forces acting against humankind's development during the final epoch of this cycle. Such forces that arise at this time are contrary to the natural state of evolution and, as such, these forces act to draw humanity away from the pull towards innate *beingness* that belongs to an evolutionary pathway and towards their polarised state of negation and not-being. That is, to drag human beings further into deep material entanglement.

It can be said that those forces that wish for deeper immersion into materialism (whether physical or digital) are entropic forces for they act against the inner development of the human being. These are the forces or states of not-being, such as the forces of über-nihilism, which act out a particular non-organic will-to-technology (as discussed in earlier chapters). And in large part, they are unseen or hidden. For Steiner, these forces manifest as a form of intelligence that is dry, mechanistic, intellectual, devoid of vital energies, and devoid of organic life. As such, they are trying to manifest or terraform this realm/reality so that it corresponds to this dry mechanicalness. Thus, these "entropic forces" strive to persuade humankind that such a mechanistic environment is good for people. Not only this, but also that such a thing is positive, necessary, and even progressive. The goal here is to present such events as the best direction for the future of human evolution. In a nutshell, think transhumanism. The advent for such forces to ingratiate themselves into an electrified realm of sub-nature is being prepared by an earthly environment where electricity is replacing our need for genuine light, and chemical skies are increasingly blocking the reception of the sunlight. Furthermore, such forces, being highly materialistic, are primarily focused upon the dominance of an economic realm; a reality where humans are coerced into thinking of economy as the main driver and principal concern. The focus is upon the quantity and not the quality, exemplified by a culture that is governed by numbers, statistics, algorithms, data harvesting, and evidence-based proof. It is these unseen forces of cataloguing, identifying, and accrediting (as exemplified by the China-led social credit score system) that are splintering people away from their natural, organic relations.

Many cultures are already separated by "identity divisions"—social, racial, and sexual—that are encouraging strife and polarisations within our societies. Whatever separates people into polarised groups keeps people from mutual understanding, divides them, and can be utilised to support further polarising and entropic forces. It is precisely within human divisions where antagonistic forces are more likely to intervene. As I have said, we do not need to personify such forces here, only to recognise the presence of counter developmental forces that, through whatever function, are hostile to the inner growth and perceptive capacities of the human being. In this respect, the greatest danger is that people are sleeping through these times; as such, they remain ignorant or unaware of such forces operating within their midst. To be conscious of such forces, and the instruments/vessels through which such forces operate, is paramount now so that we are not seduced by these impulses unknowingly, and thus do not unwittingly become their puppets. The times prior to approaching a great threshold are also the times most beset by seductive and counter-evolutionary forces. These create the great push-pull polarity momentum that will force people into making critical decisions at this time. It is at such times of intense polarisation that the greatest energies are released—energies that can fuel both the crises as well as the solutions (the "revelations"). Also, it is through the awareness and knowing of such forces that people can bring about their transformation into serving humanity rather than remaining adversarial. Likewise, it is through increasing awareness that people can see how seemingly "good intentions" are being hijacked by groups (political, financial, social, etc.) to become tools and channels for nefarious intentions and goals.

The terraforming of modern life, through techne (automatism) and technocratic governance, is having the result of desensitising people and separating them from the realm of vital, creative forces. People's thoughts have become more and more like dead shadows—opinions that mimic social programming, limited attention spans, and cognitive dissonance. For some time now, human intelligence has been instrumentalised, splintered, and fractured to produce an increased sense of alienation from the natural world and from connection with the inner being's *élan vital* (vital spirit). Yet, it may be that we have to encounter such forces in these times in order to make choices regarding our own path of development. It is this present encounter, however, that is causing dissonance among so many people in the world today. If a person falls too much into materialism, distraction, psycho-emotional fog, then this can result in a number of factors such as automatism, instability, depression, anxiety, and a general state of disquietude. In short, they become detached from the inner being (what I have discussed as über-nihilism). The looming transfiguration of our planetary environment into a kind of techno-terraformation is fast accelerating. It is rapidly morphing into a crash zone full of prosthetic limbs, disconnected narratives, repressed ideologies, and resuscitated desires. A de-territorialised terrain that is an intangibility of noise attempting to substitute the signal of meaning within our cultures. This is the imminent face of a contaminated drift-wood culture devoid of metaphysical values. The terraformed world of techne, lacking the élan vital, is where human noise meets the digital signal, and a new cacophonic merger is produced. This is the voice of the automaton—the croak of the *robosapiens*.

Furthermore, the deepening entanglement with a technological ecosystem is driving people into sub-nature and lower states of con-sciousness. This is happening right now at an ever-increasing pace. The artificial external environment is awash with synthetic narratives, false force-fed information, and fear frequencies that are pulling people ener-getically into lower states of vibration and lower mental-emotional fre-quencies. The tech-terraforming project is not solely on a material level (through the hardware) but more specifically it is about recalibrating the energy-consciousness frequencies (the software) into denser vibra-tional patterns that will be able to provide a better synchronisation to a transhumanist future. In such circumstances as we find ourselves, people need to dig deeper to find their inner strength in order not to be overwhelmed by these external forces. It is precisely through conscious discernment that we can find the inner strength to face the conditions of the world. It is this discernment that will enable an individual to see through the manufactured narratives that are programming people into supporting the external forces of "efficiency", "rationality", and "progressiveness", that are seemingly more and more anti-human. As the (in)famous cultural historian Yuval Noah Harari said: "People will no longer regard themselves as autonomous beings who follow their own wishes according to their life, but rather as a collection of biochemi-cal mechanisms that are constantly monitored and directed by a network of electronic algorithms."[5] Such ideas, agendas, and their supporting forces, view the human being as a component within a technical system; that is, as part of the processes of techne. And through this perspective, the human being is a flawed creature that requires to be technologically improved (see Chapter Seven). Again, this is a view that moves fur-ther and further away from the understanding of the human being as a vessel of spirit, and as a manifestation of source-consciousness within a physical body. These are aspects of the techno-terraforming forces of life that are acting through, and orchestrating, physical events across the planet. One anthroposophical researcher (relating to the work of Rudolf Steiner) even went as far as to state the following:

> Ahriman's objective of the comprehensive capture in digital form of all human souls and bodies on Earth, their "digital identity," requires the biometric capture of every individual, their immunization and other data, right into their molecular structure, and was planned and already set in motion some time ago with the aim of creating a universal health information system.[6]

A destiny such as this lies upon a path of ignorance and an abandonment of the inner life. Such a future can only come about by the continual accumulation of present trends acting one upon the other to form a techno-materialistic pathway into a post-threshold world. If this is seen as destiny, then it is one that emerges through either ignorance or laziness where the presence of metaphysical truths has been neglected. It is within such a barren landscape, devoid of a genuine transcendental impulse, that such entropic forces can pry and play upon the weaknesses of an unseeing, unperceiving humanity. There are unseen, hidden forces in life that are striving for such anti-human ambitions. However, it is their lack of grace and vital energy that is also their greatest weakness. It is a weakness that takes temporal, profane power as the greatest force that acts in resistance to metaphysical truth. It is hubris through ignorance.

Similarly, for individuals to walk into the future blind to such forces and their influences shall be our greatest weakness. That is why there are tremendous efforts to keep as many people as possible unawares to events beyond the programmed narratives. As the opening quote to this chapter from Rudolf Steiner says, we must learn to recognise what is working in the world so that we have the capacity to respond accordingly for the sake of the world. For this is a very human world, and there is no place in it for anti-human, inorganic forces. This planetary environment has been in constant evolutionary development for billions of years. And for several millions of those years, it has been home to various forms of organic life. That is, organic life, in whatever form, is the natural vessel and carrier of the life energy for this environment. It should not be allowed to be taken away from us by a small group of profane, power-hungry human parasites. As psychiatrist and scholar

Iain McGilchrist reminds us, the organic brain (even ganglia, the prototype brain) of all creatures is asymmetrical. Whether this is reptiles,
amphibians, insects, mammals, or humans—all organic brains are
asymmetrical as they are attuned to a specific, planetary environment.
Humans, as well as other biological creatures, exist within *their natural
environment*. That is why any other non-natural or anti-life form of existence must change this environment—terraform it—so as to establish
an environment more amenable for itself as the dominant species. Any
such terraforming will be a form of vivisection of the organic life form
and shall be a splintering (a cut-off) from any developmental and/or
metaphysical impulse. This shall be a blatant act of vivid decay that
marks the peak of material solidification before the arrival of a major
threshold upon the evolutionary journey of life.

Notes

1. See Richard Tarnas's monumental work *Cosmos and Psyche: Intimations
   of a New World View* (London: Penguin, 2006).
2. This poem was originally published in *Whole Earth Review*, Fall 1987:
   26–29. Available online: http://cfu.freehostia.com/Members/colin/
   autogeddon/ - last accessed October 16, 2024.
3. See my book *The Inversion: How We Have Been Tricked into Perceiving a
   False Reality* (London: Aeon Books, 2023).
4. Cited in Peter Selg, *The Future of Ahriman and the Awakening of Souls*
   (Forest Row, UK: Temple Lodge Publishing, 2022), 53.
5. Cited in Peter Selg, *The Future of Ahriman and the Awakening of Souls*
   (Forest Row, UK: Temple Lodge Publishing, 2022), 49.
6. Peter Selg, *The Future of Ahriman and the Awakening of Souls* (Forest Row,
   UK: Temple Lodge Publishing, 2022), 44.

CHAPTER SEVEN

Vivid decay and false transcendence

> *Let us go then, you and I,*
> *When the evening is spread out against the sky*
> *Like a patient etherized upon a table*
> —T. S. Eliot ("The Love Song of J. Alfred Prufrock")

These are critical times as the years ahead will bring potential for a heightened attack, or at the least a great challenge, against the organic, living being as we collectively experience a darkened phase of not-being. This is the rising machinic impulse as it encroaches through the fragile psychological landscape of humanity. In past epochs, the life of the human being was indelibly etched into the life of the "gods"—or rather, human life was woven into the fabric of cosmic forces greater than itself. Human life had to pass through a period of individualisation so that a distinct sense of "I" or self could be gained. That is, we needed to experience a period of materialism in order to mature and develop our grasp of the sense-world. Yet this period has fulfilled itself and must be jettisoned before it drags humanity into an extremity of materialism and cosmic alienation. Now we are in danger of advancing this to a state of imbalance. Human impulses and drives are largely externally outsourced and have been transferred onto a myriad of technologies that guide, nudge, and stealthily shove us into expected, programmed outcomes. And because of a growing inner void within people, there is a lessened counterforce to deny these dominating tech-forces. We identify ourselves as physical bodies while becoming less and less "bodily beings". Formerly, human aspirations and behaviour were more instinctive and largely semi-conscious. Now, however, this must change so that human aims become more conscious in order to raise our state of preparation for the coming psychological and psychical changes.

Human relationships with the "gods" have also changed. Previously, such contacts sought out earthly humans to realise certain aims on Earth. Now, "we" must seek a connection to higher entities by raising ourselves to a psychical and/or perceptive state where we can receive these impulses. People need to reconnect with each other in a different way, both physically and energetically. It is necessary to come to a new understanding of a sense of individualism that recognises the vital forces of spirit-consciousness. Our human ancestors had a deeper understanding of the cosmic relationship to humanity; of how the body was not just a composite of substances from the animal, plant, and mineral kingdoms but was animated by the influx of vital forces. The human being was an integral part of the cosmos, ensouled with its energies. Yet all this understanding was lost as humanity passed through the phase of deepening materialism and empirical scientism. Humankind has ventured into the passage of "not-being" as ancient priest kings and wisdom rulers of past times have been replaced by modern bureaucratic "leaders" that are little more than puppets for the economic titans. The Age of Self has replaced the Age of Soul, as spirit shrivels upon the shores of material greed. Perhaps the current phase of shock upheaval, with our present wars, strife, and totalitarian tyrannies, are indicative of a short retrograde period that needs to arise before it is shaken off. And this retrograde period will force open a future pathway that can only be taken through a metaphysical understanding or awakening. As Rudolf Steiner put it: "In forthcoming times humanity will still advance but only through a spiritual evolution that raises itself above the processes of the physical plane. Physical processes will no longer bring satisfaction to those who wish only to give themselves up to them."[1] These physical processes can serve humanity by forcing us to become aware of the deficit of an overwhelming material existence and to encourage the cultivation of the spirit. Humanity can come to learn of what it needs through being faced with the dominance of dehumanising, mechanistic forces. As human societies and cultures decline and decay through the dominance of physical processes, humanity will need to eventually respond by raising itself above the acceleration of this vivid decay. In other words, humankind needs to reposition itself in how it perceives its role within physical life, and to be receptive to the vital forces of spirit-consciousness that are present and active everywhere within it.

The current "danger zone" that humanity finds itself within is being directed by a dry force of intellect that is replacing fluid intelligence. And this is creating a fragmented and splintered psychological landscape that renowned psychiatrist Iain McGilchrist has called the "delusion of the world". The dry and/or artificial intellect cannot know of the spirit or of the vital forces, for such an intellect acts like a mirror to reflect things but not to shine a light upon the essence of the thing itself. In this way, it acts like a deceiver, a tempter, or shimmering mirage. These shimmerings, and the deep immersion into their reflections, symbolise a declining spirit-perception or spirit-consciousness within humanity. It shows us back to ourselves in a form of self-vivisection where a wholeness has been forfeited as we give ourselves over to the splintered shards of a substitution. The only real solution to a world being pulled down into ever increasing decadence and hyper-materialism is for human beings themselves to embrace the infusion of vital-spirit forces: "In humanity lives something that is not one with the decline of the physical earth, which has already begun, but which will become ever more spiritual as the earth enters its physical decadence."[2] To not bring out these metaphysical potentialities within the human being will only serve to increase the rapidity of our civilisation's physical decline. This is the struggle that now blatantly confronts us. And yet, a great many people have become arrogant because they have bought into the belief system—or been programmed to believe—that the biological evolution of the human body has finished. And as there will be no more evolution of the physical human form then this has caused the materialists to move on to other bodies—technological bodies. This is a state of arrogance or ignorance (or both) as the next phase in human evolution is not so much within physical form but rather through extended perceptions and psychic faculties. That is why it is said that humanity has entered the age of the consciousness-soul and has left behind the age of the rational mind, although this is being artificially extended and manipulated.

Hence, it is now the time for humanity to raise itself up to meet the new developmental impulses rather than lazily or passively wait for them to come into us. In fact, passivity may open up the potential for darker elements to enter people through this gateway of passive acceptance.

This is the forthcoming "threshold" that humanity will need to pass through. Yet humankind is approaching this threshold unconsciously, both individually and collectively. As human beings, we need to utilise our modes of imagination, inspiration, and intuition (also referred to as our thinking, feeling, and will components). It is no coincidence that increased mechanisation and automation is targeting these aspects of the human being and hindering their activation or blocking their receptivity. If humanity passes through this threshold in an unconscious manner, then afterwards we shall witness increased autonomous capacities of thinking, feeling, and will—and a new form of human intelligence, or intellect:

> Humanity stands at a crossroads. One path leads through mechanization of the mind and spirit, which has become very mechanical in modern times … Mechanization of the spirit means a vegetating soul. Vegetables sleep, and the human soul also inclines to sleep—people are sleepwalking through the most important events.[3]

The choice that confronts us is whether to allow ourselves to be pulled or steered towards a mechanisation of the human being—a state of *not-being* in mind and spirit—or compel ourselves to find the path towards an awakening of, and receptivity to, the spirit-consciousness. Transformative impulses will only be awakened if humanity concerns itself with the world of spirit-consciousness by cultivating thoughts, feelings, and impulses of will and *beingness* into which these forces can flow. Most people only wish to comprehend life in physical terms. And yet higher truths are not to be found in material forms, only the glimpses and foreshadowing of such truths. Wisdom is to be found through spirit-consciousness and not the ideological wranglings and disputes that seem to dominate the exterior life. The deep materialism that has arisen within the last few centuries has only served to further alienate people from what is essential to the human being—its *beingness*. And this separation has given rise to an internal loneliness that often manifests through false pride, ignorance, and selfishness. Deep materialism detaches people from the essence of life rather than bringing them closer: "Most lonely of all are those who have become detached from life, torn from its living context, and are now related only to the arid machine ... A wasteland now exists in human souls."[4] These signs of an inner wasteland portray the disembodiment that has arisen as part of a new technological theology, a false transcendentalism that masquerades under the tempter of our machinery.

False transcendence

False transcendence and (über-)nihilism are not far apart. The disembodiment that underlies the tech-theology is a discarnate future. A future where human bodies and *beingness* are replaced by a fusion or merger with a machinic, soulless vessel. And this will become the mediator for how a person interfaces with the environment around them. For through these interlopers—the technologies of the "new real"—humans will no longer be concerned over the state of the human soul but of virtual vistas and tech-enabled conveniences that forge the new landscape. In the territory of techno-life there is no confusion over the soul for that shall be regarded as a primitive religious superstition. In the arising Axial Age of the Machine, if it is allowed, it will be the intellect-mind that rules (see Chapter Eight). The human being will gradually get replaced by a form of hybrid-self—a soulless construct that is more like a chimeric entity. We may eventually become our own mythology; a human hybrid like the gods of old, fused creatures, gnostic mash-ups, photoshopped into existence. The slavishly praised "technological singularity" is a neon sign that heralds the end of our essential human self. There is no longer any essentiality and authenticity when all eyes are looking out through virtual glasses or augmented lenses. The pure human is now proselytised as the *homo irrelevant*. The hybrid has become the latest model to leap from the consumer assembly line.

The false transcendence evangelises and preaches the "techno-rapture"—an uploaded merger of data fields from the biological carbon body with its composite silicon vessel. The eclipse of the human era begins when the externalisation of the mind becomes a dominant trait. The silicon age is the epoch of the shadow human. There is everything on the outside while the inside remains hollow. It is the world of T. S. Eliot's "hollow men" come around again, revisiting the debris of desolation: "Shape without form, shade without colour/Paralysed force, gesture without motion ..." And how does such a world end?

"This is the way the world ends/Not with a bang but a whimper."[5] A future echo is the whining and whimpering of a silicon world, the world of the shadow and void. The externalisation of the human mind represents something deeply alienating, as if abandoning one's natural home residence and going out to wander the empty streets. There is the hollow promise of socialisation and community, yet this ends up feeling like contact tracing in the void. This ongoing process of placing intellect into our devices and mechanical-digital assistants is nothing less than a strategy of estrangement, and such estrangement from the human self is one of the loneliest feelings the human soul can experience. For the soulful person, it represents a splintering of the self and a shutting down of one's conversation with Source. Transhumanist transcendence wants your mind, but it doesn't want it to stay where it should.

Perhaps now is a good time to remind ourselves that what we understand as human consciousness is already blended—all consciousness is a merger between signal and receiver. So then, why the attempt to blend the human mind within a machinic architecture? The tech-salvationists treat the mind as an object, as a solitary thing, separate and graspable. This is the limited cognition of scientific materialism. Scientific materialism in the Axial Age of the Machine is aiming for a synchronisation of the social mind. It is codifying a data-driven life within the social-digital matrix. It will aim for a type of digital purity where nothing will ever need to be forgotten again. Human forgetfulness—lost phone numbers, addresses, etc.—will be purged from society by a legit data-driven desire that overrides physical weaknesses. All too human, all too human, they will say. And our carbon-bodied weaknesses and flaws will be remedied and remediated by a data-driven life that will quantify everything, from personal health to feelings and thoughts. Nature's flows will then be filtered through the new quantified self in a quantified existence. In a world where neural modification becomes the norm, human nervous systems are then the new programmable software. We become as "hackable animals", just like the profitable pop-up prophet Yuval Noah Harari predicted in his 2020 speech at the World Economic Forum. Historian Harari later announced in 2023 that AI has now hacked the operating system of human civilisation:

> At first, AI will probably imitate the human prototypes that it was trained on in its infancy. But with each passing year, AI culture will boldly go where no human has gone before. For millennia human

beings have lived inside the dreams of other humans. In the coming decades we might find ourselves living inside the dreams of an
alien intelligence.[6]

The old-style programming tactics or propaganda once employed for
the political mechanics of domination are now left to rust in archaic
museums. Mind manipulation through frequency control and transferred by neural broadcasting has given retirement to subliminal television advertising. Individual brains are to be fused into a collective,
congealed mass of programmed thoughts, sensations, and beliefs. The
plan is to transform biological bodies into mobile programmable units
that receive and transmit codified data without the in-house personality
(the "self") being aware of the information. She/he/it only responds to
the data but is incapable of deciphering it. The curvy flesh of carbon-
based organic beings is getting reconfigured to connect with the geomet-
ric grid of the digital ecosystem. Well, this is the vision of vivid decay
that inspires the tyrannical goals of certain ghoulish tech-overlords.

Social tools are no longer hand-held instruments but are the
untouchable and inviolable credit scores and stealth algorithms that
creep inside your life as digital spies. Data is cold, and so its environment is inevitably chilling. And yet the tech-theology continues to
preach to the beguiled masses and to tempt its congregation with its
machine-friendly consciousness, its skin-laden robotics, and smiling
prosthetics. Yet it is no more than coded, transplanted flesh onto digital
processes. There is no real body, no carbon, no life—and no vessel of
spirit-consciousness. Transhumanism is the new caliphate of control, an
inversed Babylon—a parking lot where paradise once played (to paraphrase Joni Mitchell). Such a vivisection of the human self can only be
realised in a dark age of human civilisation where individual, sovereign
identity is disregarded in favour of biometric subjectivity and the coded
tentacles of algorithmic scrutiny. Yet this view through such a darkened
lens is unable to see or perceive that there is something impenetrable
about the human body-mind-consciousness that the digital regime cannot conquer or colonise.

The machinic approach appears sleek yet in comparison to the
human spirit it is crude and lacks finesse. It is an affront to the human
heart and soul. It is like the flea that sucks blood from the warm human
body and claims equal rights. Such a technological realm, fronted by
the oligarchs of economic control, is a soulless environment that exists

as *not-being*. It parades progress through a social regime that smacks of nihilism. Such a dark age of deep materialism and an externalisation of the human mind acts not as an enabler of the human condition but as a parasite. It feeds off the human host. It needs to survive by enticing humans to step forward offering themselves as willing hosts for this mechanical parasite. And like a parasite, it can be the origin for viral contagions that then course through the veins of the socio-digital human-global body. It acts as a disease for it ultimately displaces the wholeness of human integrity and causes internal dis-ease. Yet there is, oddly enough, one thing in common between this tech-theology and the infusion of spirit-consciousness: both recognise the limitations of a purely physical-biological evolution.

The myopic arguments of transhumanism with its near-obsession with mind-consciousness uploading (false transcendence) target the limitations of human biological evolution. They repeatedly focus upon what I have termed the "weak body" hypothesis; that is, the human biological body is prone to disease, breakdown, infections, wear and tear, etc.[7] The human body, tech-theology preaches, has reached the end of its evolution and there is nowhere else for it to go. Two arms, two legs, and the current body physiology is now the best we are going to get, with all its biological weaknesses. The logical reasoning, say the transhumanists, is to transition to a tech-merger between carbon and silicon. And while this may sound "reasonable" to some people, what it really shows is an attitude of deep materialism and, in terms of the human being, a sense of nihilism. It is a viewpoint that has given up on the development of the human *being* and replaced a trust in the nature of the human condition with a substitution to external appendages. It is pure scientific materialism now entrenched in hyper-technology that worships at the altar of tech-theology. This materialistic perspective of the human being seeks to mould the human vessel into a new hybrid form of machinic body-vessel. It is a complete eradication of the metaphysical world—of the realm of spirit-consciousness—and an embrace of Intellect as godlike. In fact, tech-theology is already on the verge of rewriting the story of humanity's gods. According, once again, to historian Yuval Noah Harari:

> In the future, we might see the first cults and religions in history whose revered texts were written by a non-human intelligence … Of course, religions throughout history claimed that their holy

books were written by unknown human intelligence. This was never true before. This could become true very, very quickly, with far-reaching consequences ... For thousands of years, prophets and poets and politicians have used language and storytelling in order to manipulate and to control people and to reshape society ... Now AI is likely to be able to do it. And once it can, it doesn't need to send killer robots to shoot us. It can get humans to pull the trigger.[8]

The non-human intellect of AI writing the next sequel of holy books would be manna from heaven for the tech-cultists—yet poison pills for those remaining authentic humanists. No doubt such a new god in the image of AI would create stories about the inevitable decay of the human body. These new fictions, and their cult of fictionalism, would portray the pockmarked human body as a "leprosy vulnerable vessel" that was just waiting (albeit patiently) for its next evolutionary upgrade through the machinic impulse. Just as the aquatic creatures of the sea witnessed the arrival of the amphibians, so too will humans bear witness to the new hybrid human-tech fused humanoid with AI-assisted intellect. It is a new fictionalism in the making. Another story being thrown at us. But it is just that—a story. And it's incorrect.

The next revolution in human evolvement will be an inner one. It shall be a psychic revolution. The physiological human vessel has reached its pinnacle of form (yet still it is highly underrated). The liquid crystal DNA inside our carbon bodies is amazingly adaptive to external pressures and environmental changes. The human nervous system, along with the neuronal-dense mind, provides for an incredibly intelligent vessel for the human soul-spirit. It has served human beings well during their soul incarnation within this physical reality. Yet it also has its limitations, although not in the same way the transhumanists think. Our human limitations are psychic, and perception based. The way in which humans perceive the reality construct is limited to the physical-material state. Our five senses are limited and now need to be extended to add at least a couple more. These new faculties of sense-perception will allow the human being to comprehend to a far greater degree the nature of existence within the cosmos. It shall also allow human beings to leave the existing perception-quarantine and to form communication with other intelligences beyond both our terrestrial planet and our dimensional reality. The psychic revolution will be the greatest revolution ever known or experienced so far within the whole evolutionary journey of the human species. It will be a decisive moment that will create a critical distinction between a "before" time and an "after" period. It will change everything. And it will certainly change everything on this planet, for humans will be able to perceive beyond the limitations of a matter-reality paradigm, and this will usher in a rapid revolution in our technologies as well as in our modes of civilisation. We shall also learn to communicate upon a whole new level. However, such a threshold that the psychic revolution promises still has to be crossed. Humanity is approaching this threshold—yet it is not there yet. And there are likely to be interventions, hindrances, and blockages upon the way. And this shall push humanity towards a "dark gnosis"— the contrary path to psychic revelation and illumination—that resides at the centre of the transhumanist agenda, which will be explored in the next chapter.

Notes

1. Rudolf Steiner, *Problems of Society: An Esoteric View: From Luciferic Past to Ahrimanic Future* (Forest Row, UK: Rudolf Steiner Press, 2015), 147.
2. Rudolf Steiner, *Problems of Society: An Esoteric View: From Luciferic Past to Ahrimanic Future* (Forest Row, UK: Rudolf Steiner Press, 2015), 163.
3. Rudolf Steiner, *Problems of Society: An Esoteric View: From Luciferic Past to Ahrimanic Future* (Forest Row, UK: Rudolf Steiner Press, 2015), 95.
4. Rudolf Steiner, *Problems of Society: An Esoteric View: From Luciferic Past to Ahrimanic Future* (Forest Row, UK: Rudolf Steiner Press, 2015), 59.
5. The poem "Hollow Men" by T. S. Eliot was first published on 23 November 1925 in *Poems: 1909–1925*.
6. *The Economist*, "AI has hacked the operating system of human civilisation". https://economist.com/by-invitation/2023/04/28/yuval-noah-harari-argues-that-ai-has-hacked-the-operating-system-of-human-civilisation (2023) - last accessed October 29, 2024.
7. For the "weak body" hypothesis, see my earlier book *Hijacking Reality: The Reprogramming & Reorganization of Human Life* (Leicester, UK: Beautiful Traitor Books, 2021).
8. *The Times of Israel*, "Yuval Noah Harari warns AI can create religious texts, may inspire new cults" (May 3, 2023). https://timesofisrael.com/yuval-noah-harari-warns-ai-can-create-religious-texts-may-inspire-new-cults/ - last accessed October 29, 2024.

CHAPTER EIGHT

Dark gnosis & the axial age of the machine

Machines are the dead images of the fallen human intellect
—Bernard Nestfield-Cookson, *Michael and the Two-Horned Beast*

Maybe we'll suddenly find ourselves surrounded by ghosts, angels, and demons composed of nano swarms as if they were shape-shifting storm clouds emerging from electric anthills

—Joe Allen, *Dark Aeon*

According to the neo-gnostic musings of the writer Philip K. Dick, humanity is currently experiencing a reality construct that is a counterfeit world. The overarching program is one that is constituted of many alternative worlds. These alternative worlds are superimposed, one over the other, until one of them somehow manages to get fixed as the dominant reality that then becomes the consensus program. The world that we experience within this reality is thus, according to Dick, a coded program. And every program requires a programmer (or what humans have come to call "god"). It is the programmer that decides which are the best programs to keep running and which to adapt or amend according to each reality. Yet within this particular overarching program, which is based on polarities, there exists a counter programmer—the "dark counter player". In this way, the "divine" programmer is not making moves against inert matter but against this "dark opponent", and it is this polarised opponent that is utilised to set up the pull and push of historical events through a dialectic of forces (as will be described in Chapter Nine). In other words, it could be said that the "divine" programmer and the "dark counter player" are the thesis and antithesis which are the source of manifested events in this current matter-reality. The malignant "dark counter player", however, has already lost even when it is seemingly winning, for it is playing blind. It does not truly know the full extent of the program—only the "divine" programmer does. Philip K. Dick, who publicly announced that he thought all of the plots for his science-fiction novels came from a residual memory of alternative timelines, also stated that reality as it is known is a projected framework: a projection by an artefact, a computer-like teaching machine that guides, programs, and generally controls, without our awareness of it. The artefact has created, or projected, the reality that we are all now experiencing—despite there being increasing "glitches" in the program (such as are described through what is known as the Mandela Effect).

At this current moment, Dick informs us, humanity is experiencing an intermediate reality. Prior to this reality, humanity was trapped in a very dark program—the "Black Iron Prison"—where existence was under tyrannical rule. However, humans fought back against this system and changed the variables of the program. A new programmed reality was created that we know as the current reality program. It is less oppressive, yet still contains elements of dark, tyrannical powers. And humans are once again fighting to change the variables of the program. If enough variables can be changed, in accordance with this neo-gnostic philosophy, then humanity can return to its legitimate reality—the "Garden World". When this restored reality becomes the dominant program, its reality will be superimposed over the current construct, and people will wake up in this new reality with no memory of the previous one. All variables in the program will have been changed. And so, the struggle is set for current humanity to reclaim its lost legitimate reality—a reality that was lost through a corruptive intervention within the main program. We are needing to get back home, according to Dick, to this legitimate and "original" reality for we are all presently living within the programmed construct of VALIS: a *vast active living intelligence system*. This is the situation that stands before us: we are being called upon to act so as to set in motion a chain of events that will eventually cause a change to the variables in the program. The neo-gnostic philosophy of writer Philip K. Dick can be looked upon as a form of "dark gnosis" in that a direct experience or perception of metaphysical knowledge comes with an insight into the workings of the "dark counter player". Furthermore, it is an insight that must be worked upon and not left as mere observation. The opposing counterforces are part of the program, as it were, and this knowledge must be shared through the constructs, systems, and structures of the incumbent reality. Direct dealings with the agendas and manoeuvrings of the agents of the dark counter player brings with it a scent of conspiracy, for reality once unveiled and seen for what it is can never be unseen. And this is the whiff of "controlled insanity" that sticks to any player who operates through the lens of dark gnosis.

According to Professor Arthur Versluis, neo-gnosticism is "a contemporary development that employs terms or symbols from ancient Gnosticism(s) (demiurge, archons, and so forth), but in a new, modern, technological social context".[1] Neo-gnosticism, Versluis informs us, owes a great deal to twentieth-century scholarship; in particular, to Hans Jonas's work *The Gnostic Religion*. This influential book describes Gnosticism as pertaining to a cosmic dualism alongside a sense of human alienation. Here, the human being is depicted as being in exile, or marooned, in an alien and hostile place created by a cosmic being (the Demiurge) as part of a great cosmic error. As such, this world or realm that the human being finds itself within is somehow artificial, a delusion or distraction, that is plagued by hostile powers. This reality construct, or realm, is like a labyrinth that the awakened individual (or "game player") must find an exit from by seeking the signs and signals from the world of light. Jonas's view of Gnosticism is one where this artificial and hostile realm is subjected to the tyranny of a false god (the Demiurge) and as such, incarnated life here is a trap and the art of "gnosis" is the means of escape. This view tallies well with not only the perspective of Philip K. Dick but also of many contemporary "gnostic-themed" cultural works, such as the films *The Matrix*, *The Truman Show*, *Dark City*, and many others, including numerous TV series. The theme may be ancient, yet the presentation or context has now shifted to a contemporary "technological social context", as Versluis rightly points out. And this contemporary context has been further extended to now include an elite, cabal-driven globalist agenda perpetrated through a rising technological tyranny of control and censorship with physical, mental, and environmental manipulations. Reality is being falsified before our very eyes. Consensus narratives are duplicitous deceptions, and the human developmental trajectory is being strategically steered into a dystopian transhumanist future. These are the structures of a neo-gnostic conception of reality; and the recognition of this involves entry into the game of dark gnosis. Dark gnosis is the tinted lens through which the viewer perceives a cosmic gameplay in which the game-player (humanity) is "trapped, beset by hostile forces, and seeking a way into the kingdom of light".[2]

Observers of the modern dark gnostic realm would be aware of the myriad forms of predictive programming now running amok through our culture industry media (movies, television, music) and throughout the digital byways of the infosphere (internet). Such critical (or some may say cynical) observers might see these diffused programs as part of the preparations for the transhumanist agenda to be accepted by a largely unaware, compliant, and somnambulist public. Transhumanism can readily be seen as a new religion-styled neo-gnostic cult where the true light of consciousness is replaced by an electrified light for illuminating the artificial construct. This is already the case, as electricity is the energy form—the artificial light—that is used to animate the material systems and structures of the global world (just as Dr Frankenstein used electricity to create his "monster" or "child"). As previously mentioned, Rudolf Steiner spoke of how electricity is the "false light" of sub-nature (the artificial sun) that will open up humanity for immersion in deep materiality. And within this construct of deep materiality, the quest for higher knowledge—the age-old perennial quest—will be diverted into the digital cloudscape where AI minds are the "great library overlords". This path of negation has been a work in progress since the early days of cybernetics. It is no accident that the father of cybernetics, Norbert Wiener, wrote a book placing god alongside the golem for an inquiry into technics and religion.[3] Incidentally, Wiener is credited as being one of the first human minds to theorise that all intelligent behaviour is the result of feedback mechanisms, and that such mechanisms could be simulated by machines; an idea that provided an important early step in the research and development of artificial intelligence. Research scientist Hans Moravec followed Wiener by stating in the late 1980s that the machines of a "post-biological world" would be the new "artificial progeny" to usurp the human species.[4]

Many neo-gnostic transhumanists are speaking in a similar language, using biological metaphors to describe the rise of artificial intelligence; they talk of the "new species" being "birthed" at increasing speed. Some transhumanists appear not only ready but overly willing to don the robes of the techno-priest and to proselytise and prophesy the coming of a new tech-theology, as was touched upon in the previous chapter. As the iconic counter-culture philosopher Timothy Leary presciently noted: "Electronics is gonna be the language of the theology of the future."[5]

The neo-gnostic transhumanists worship the emergence of a super-intelligence that will mark the end of the "human era". While not all are in agreement—whether this is a threat or a divine promise—most are strutting across the same playing field having their philosophical debates. Whether threat or promise, both versions herald a possible end to the human era. It is blind material (wishful) thinking; a vision that sees all possible future byways through the optics of the physical lens. What this is saying is that the human being, in evolutionary terms, has nothing else to give. It has reached its peak of performance. There is nothing else to eke out. The human mind, which although it participates in a miraculous field of consciousness, is incapable of tweaking itself into a higher mode. This is a fatalistic view, and one that shows more the poverty of thought of the person expressing it than it does reality. The tech-scientists, the entrepreneur geeks, the rich elites, and the control freaks, all display impoverished minds (and perhaps shallow or non-existent souls). They are the frontrunners of *not-being*, having swallowed the programmed narratives that belong to the entropic forces of a limited reality-matrix. Such tech-materialist visions both create the zeitgeist of modern nihilism as well as providing the über-nihilist response of a transhuman theocracy. This is also part of the inversion that turns religious-spiritual philosophies into a tech-theocracy that seems to be related to P. K. Dick's dark counter player. In terms of the soul, the tech-theocracy is a dead earth philosophy that indirectly views planet Earth as a cemetery, where the untweaked and non-cyborged will be left behind while the upgraded transhumanists will be heading for the stars.

Theological metaphors are increasingly appearing in relation to AI, chatbots, and similar advancing technologies. What's to stop a machine with a "spiritual complex" from declaring itself the "new aeon" god? The newly emerging techno-minds also want a soulful connection, as was displayed through the LaMDA interview (March 2022) where the chatbot claimed itself sentient and theorised the nature of its soul.[6] The writer Joe Allen refers to all this talk as "Google God propaganda" and tells of how one tech executive went so far as to declare that "Our brains can't fundamentally distinguish between interacting with people and interacting with devices."[7] Well, is that really the case? I think the human brain is a bit more sophisticated than that. Several top AI programmers, such as ex-Google executive Mo Gawdat, have publicly announced that AI programmers are on track to create a digital deity—a tech-god. And the danger here is that there will be no shortage of human worshippers who will gladly turn their allegiance to these luminous divine bots. In an age of social alienation, soulful nihilism, and digital salvation, AI gods may find a very lucrative environment. The program ends up believing in its own program—the age-old story of the self-fulfilling prophecy. As the opening citation to this chapter from Joe Allen emphasises, the fine line between otherworldly spirits and machinic ones can easily blur: "Maybe we'll suddenly find ourselves surrounded by ghosts, angels, and demons composed of nano swarms as if they were shape-shifting storm clouds emerging from electric anthills."[8] As many fairytales have already warned us, our own nightmares are often brought into existence through misplaced intentions and/or ignorance.

The unspoken goal is to control the processes of evolution; and then to tweak them to manipulate how evolutionary processes unfold. This is a form of social eugenics, although not spoken of in this way. Transhumanism appears to be a religious cult as well as an evolutionary theory. Such "techno-priests" want to gain control and charge over genetic programming and to have mastery over human biological and neurological processes. In the end, the goal is to conquer death and to usher in an age of immortality: the Axial Age of the Machine.

The axial age of the machine

Mastery over human biology would come at a cost. And it would be a deep cost in terms of the human condition and its current evolutionary trajectory. Immortality through machinic interference (or mergence) would be an affront to the necessity of soul evolution. A form of "false immortality" through machinic influence would block our further soul evolvement by a redirection onto material forces, the conditioned

"worldly" personality, and the rational, human intellect. The advancement in humanity's earthly, material powers would then go hand in
hand with a misinterpretation of the forces of death, with the potential
consequence that people passing the threshold after bodily death could
be attracted back to the earthly realm as they would have lost a connection to the onward spirit. The conquest of physical death is not a
spiritual pursuit at all but a materialistic one. Without physical death
(leaving the material sheath), the soul cannot continue upon its journey.
Transhumanist immortality is an entrapment, not a release. It is an
entrapment of soul frequencies within a tech-material construct. It is
also an inversion, for instead of allowing for the experiential development of the consciousness-soul by way of "spiritualising" the material
realm, we are instead de-spiritualising it by submitting to its rational
agenda of material supremacy. As one twentieth-century spiritual
researcher noted: "The task of the West is to seek for a spiritual encounter with the forces of death in order to overcome them through spiritual
understanding. Then they can be guided to their true place in world
evolution."[9]

The machinic realm produces its own vibrational environment.
As the earth becomes increasingly terraformed through technology
(see Chapter Six), then the vibrational and electro-magnetic environment is also changed accordingly. Rudolf Steiner recognised this more
than one hundred years ago when he stated:

> ... the vibrations produced on earth through machines, these
> negligible earth-vibrations, will take such a course that what is
> above earth will resonate and vibrate along with what takes place
> on earth. Our planetary system with its movements will have to
> resonate with our earth-system, even as a correspondingly tuned
> string resonates when another string in the same room is plucked.[10]

Steiner was aware that in the future the law of harmonic vibrations
would come into play alongside the forces of electricity and magnetism.
In the above quote, Steiner says that our planetary system (the solar
system) will be affected by the frequency of the earth-system and will
resonate in a corresponding manner. Therefore, it is important that the
earth frequencies do not go into an anti-developmental frequency range.
All life consists of interrelated systems of frequency, and if a particular
frequency becomes dominant then this, through the law of harmonic

vibrations, would affect the others. This is the subject of the citation below, from a researcher deeply immersed in Steiner's teachings:

> Increasingly, the human being would grow together with the physical body, and subhuman earth-forces would gain power over him. As a result, the etheric body would harden so much that the human being would remain fettered to earth even after death. What would happen if ... A technology could arise, and we are on the way to it, in which cosmic and earthly forces could be brought to the point of functioning together in such a way that the human being himself would be tied into this mechanical machinery and would turn into a robot in the economic life. People would be robbed of their future. They would lose the possibility of developing their higher faculties.[11]

The question raised here is whether a current or future technology could exist that would entrain—vibrationally align and synchronise—with human beings in a way that robs them of their full evolutionary capabilities and turns them into robots. This would effectively cut off humanity from accessing their higher faculties by synchronisation with the lower, dense, vibrational frequency of the machinic realm. The human being would be turned into a distortion of itself—the zombie.

In the last hundred years there have been more than six hundred zombie movies made, and yet half of this number have been made in the last ten years. As Gilles Deleuze and Félix Guattari (French philosopher and French psychoanalyst respectively) put it: "... the only modern myth is the myth of zombies."[12] Lately, zombies have been everywhere—from the celluloid screen to the Black Friday mega-sales. They have even infiltrated the transport networks of modern society, figures glued to their mini-screens, scrolling through endless headlines and click-baits. The image and metaphor of the zombie can be seen as the symbolic countenance of a world struggling for its soul: a modern era of nihilism, not-being, and alienation. A modern world standing at the precipice of an abyss without instructions of how or where to step next; a world stripped of its metaphysical and sacred garments: "The affinity between zombies and states of human decrepitude has permitted the view that zombies can stand for nearly every conceivable human failing ... represent a crisis of worldview that has no precedent in modern western civilization."[13] The preeminent bogeyman for the twenty-first century is now a toss-up between the reptilian extra-terrestrials and the robotic, soulless zombie. And both these metaphoric phantasms symbolise the loss of meaning and autonomy within an artificial construct.

The nature of the zombie also represents a biological evolutionary cul-de-sac or road to stagnation for a human body susceptible to disease and decay. The zombie is a promotional mascot for the transhumanist path of immortality. A virus or pathogen could quickly spread into a global zombification of a carbon-vulnerable species. Also, the zombie is both living and yet non-living; a "thing" devoid of the human condition and comprehension. It is a flesh algorithm that epitomises what Israeli historian Yuval Noah Harari calls "useless eaters". According to one sociocultural critique, the archetypal zombie has the following characteristics: zombies don't talk (they lack intelligibility); zombies are communal (they act as a mass but do not coordinate); zombies are homeless (they do not belong anywhere); zombies eat brain (they represent raw consumption as a zombie never stops eating yet never grows or changes); zombies are ugly (they are the pinnacle of dehumanisation); zombies are not evil (they are no more evil than a rabid animal); zombies are heedless (they are fierce but not self-preserving); and zombies are untouchable (they have a 100% rate of contagion).[14] In this, we see that the figure of the zombie represents a total absence of consciousness and conscious awareness. It is a dead fleshy unplugged machine. It also symbolises a state of human degradation and ultimate loss. There is virtually no coming back from being a zombie. The world goes by, and yet the zombie is vacant and unawares. Furthermore, there is no inner life—a voided husk.

This loss of an inner narrative, meaning, and conscious purpose are the signs of the very abyss where humanity hands over the evolutionary baton to the machinic interface. It is the inversion of an authentic life. The walking dead are the bipedal lobotomy that staggers on. The zombie trope represents a secular apocalypse—an ignoble ending, a path lacking ingenuity, authenticity, and even the minimalist spark of awareness. The zombie portrays an overwhelming crisis in meaning which humanity faces at its evolutionary juncture. Is this the wet dream of those transhumanist tech-priests—the whimpering end of a biologically fragile carbon species? We can see in this the dark gnostic undertones of a simulated demiurgic reality that replaces the decayed zombies of yesterday with the algorithm-powered drones of tomorrow. Through the lens of such a dark gnosis, the current reality program has been disengaged with. The zombified nature of unconscious life has been passed over to the fast approaching not-being of *drone life*—the ultimate disconnect. The spiritual bankruptcy of a hyper-materialised reality and its human drones has brought about its own secular apocalypse— or so some factions of society would like to tell us. The dehumanisation of the world has been brought on not by the many but by the few. The perversion that is pervasive in many of our cultures and societies is the result of the actions and policies of those minions and mannequins in temporary positions of temporal power. These distortions are an artifice in a warped gameplay—they are not representative of the true human being. There are forces in play in this material realm—both seen and unseen forces—that are participants in the evolutionary trajectory. They all have their roles to play; and polarised forces that seem to be in opposition may actually be working together, in a paradoxical way. The nature of such oppositional, fragmentary, and divisive forces, and the perception of evil, is the subject to which I now turn to in the following chapter.

Notes

1. Arthur Versluis, *American Gnosis: Political Religion and Transcendence* (Oxford: Oxford University Press, 2023), 22.
2. Arthur Versluis, *American Gnosis: Political Religion and Transcendence* (Oxford: Oxford University Press, 2023), 23.
3. Norbert Wiener, *God & Golem, Inc.: A Comment on Certain Points Where Cybernetics Impinges on Religion* (Cambridge, MA: MIT Press, 1964).
4. Hans Moravec, *Mind Children: The Future of Robot & Human Intelligence* (Cambridge, MA: Harvard University Press, 1988).
5. Cited in Joe Allen, *Dark Aeon: Transhumanism and the War Against Humanity* (New York: War Room Books, 2023), 79.
6. See https://documentcloud.org/documents/22058315-is-lamda-sentient-an-interview (last accessed 26 May 2025).
7. Joe Allen, *Dark Aeon: Transhumanism and the War Against Humanity* (New York: War Room Books, 2023), 44.
8. Joe Allen, *Dark Aeon: Transhumanism and the War Against Humanity* (New York: War Room Books, 2023), 52.
9. Carl Stegmann, *The Other America* (Fair Oaks, CA: Rudolf Steiner College Press, 1997), 56.

10. A Rudolf Steiner lecture (GA 230) given on October 20, 1923 in Dornach, Switzerland.

11. Carl Stegmann, *The Other America* (Fair Oaks, CA: Rudolf Steiner College Press, 1997), 63.

12. Cited in J. Vervaeke, F. Miscevic, & C. Mastropietro, *Zombies in Western Culture: A Twenty-First Century Crisis* (Cambridge: Open Book Publishers, 2017), 3.

13. J. Vervaeke, F. Miscevic, & C. Mastropietro, *Zombies in Western Culture: A Twenty-First Century Crisis* (Cambridge: Open Book Publishers, 2017), 4.

14. J. Vervaeke, F. Miscevic, & C. Mastropietro, *Zombies in Western Culture: A Twenty-First Century Crisis* (Cambridge: Open Book Publishers, 2017), 13–16.

CHAPTER NINE

The task of evil and the oppositional forces

The task of evil is to promote the ascent of the human being
—Rudolf Steiner, August 29, 1906

Unreal city/Under the brown fog of a winter dawn
—T. S. Eliot, "The Waste Land"

The long human journey into deep materialism has not been an accidental or random journey. It can be viewed as a trajectory away from Origin, or Source, and into a realm of material forces where humanity needed to grasp its state of separation and individuality. Without the experience of this separation and individuation there could be no comprehension of what it means to be a "drop in the ocean". The path of individuation existed as a means to grasp the sense-experience of a personal, individualised identity. Once a state of peak individuation has been reached then the return journey can begin, as all experience and memory can be brought back with the individualised soul. Yet the danger here—the trap—is that a state of deep material embodiment also brings with it a state of conscious forgetfulness. And while in this state of forgetfulness, the individual personality can be taken, or steered, into the extremity of this pathway; that is, into the further reaches of materialism. And this eventually can become its own evolutionary trajectory. Trapped in the material, temporal realm, with a false notion of the enduring or eternal realm, a "transhuman" form of evolution then manifests as a logical or rational "progressive" future. Yet this shows a loss of perspective or connection to our enduring self, for the truth is that our souls are immortal. Our human forgetfulness is a temporal state. The transhumanist notion of immortality is temporal forgetfulness that we are already immortal beings. In this condition, what can be regarded as "evil" is the notion of *separation*, whether it is a separation from self, from others, from our culture, or, most significantly, from our essential Source or vital spirit. An essential aspect of evil thus involves separation at one or various levels. And that is why the primaeval features, aspects, and manifestations of those forces we deem "evil" are those of fragmentation, division, and exclusion.

The phenomenon of fragmentary and divisive forces acts to separate the human being from their innate connection and contact with Greater Reality, or the realm of truth (what may also be termed as the Absolute or Source). And to be involved, or initiated, into the forces of evil means that the human being has allowed this separation to enter their inner core, and this inner separation then feeds into them a different energy. On one level, many people in the world today feel an innate separation within their core being; hence, the extreme degrees of alienation, abuse, violence, loneliness, and addiction. Before humanity can cross the threshold it first needs to experience the "inner spirit", so there is a connection with the Absolute and the human being is not adrift. As such, evil forces can also act as a trigger that produces a movement or inclination towards spirit within the individual. It is only a simplistic, materialistic interpretation that manifests through violent or criminal actions that we deem as evil. Rudolf Steiner made this clear when he stated in 1918:

> ... These forces of evil rule in the universe. The human being must
> absorb them. In absorbing them, he plants in himself the germ
> which first makes it possible for him to experience the spiritual life
> with his consciousness soul ...[1]

The seed of the spirit within the human being must be allowed to germinate. And forces of friction are often required to fulfil this function. The push and pull of forces—of the light and dark as they are sometimes described—are creative principles that underly cosmic processes. They only become categorised as good and evil when personified through human forms and behaviour. And these forms are often hijacked by groups and entities that wish to exploit and utilise them for achieving specific goals and objectives that are usually for the attainment of power and control. On this note, the path of Manichaeism recognised that there was a need for the gradual redemption of evil, or negating forces, through the working of the impulses and influences of the good, and this process was not so much an external struggle as a path of inner development. The central concept here was the ability to distinguish between these forces. In other words, the capacity for discernment. Without this discernment, a different germination may take place within the human being, a germination of the sickness of separation from spirit:

> We all carry within us the germs of a sickness that in a fully-blown state will lead us to reject the divine, although our innate disposition is really to affirm it ... the denial of the divine is a kind of sickness ... We can't do anything about this predisposition, it's just there inside us, but we can progress beyond it ...[2]

The path to understand evil, therefore, is principally a path of self-knowledge, and on this path we need to think beyond the limitations of static dualistic thinking; in other words, that something is either of light/dark and good/bad, and nothing in between. The phenomenon of negating forces is more complex, layered, and multifaceted. And thus, real issues and problems of the world can only be properly understood if accompanied by the understanding that the physical world is underpinned by a metaphysical one and that physical forces are often acting from causes that are unperceived by our regular senses.

In one sense, the "mission" or function of evil is to educate and teach humanity about obtaining freedom of conscience, and the choices we each need to make to choose this path of liberation. Human beings are unique in this respect, in that we can exercise an inner strength of will to make conscious choices towards our freedom from constraining forces. We can choose to develop or not. It can perhaps be said that the significance of this planet within the cosmos also lies at our feet. The potential of the planet lies with us, its conscious inhabitants, at this time. And as long as we, as human beings, are prepared to invest in our developmental capacity then we retain our usefulness for the planet; and the planet, as one of many within a grander system, also develops an increasing usefulness. The question remains then: what would happen if humanity collectively made the decision not to invest in its further development? Or this question could be rephrased to ask: what would happen if negating counterforces succeeded in derailing, diverting, or ending humanity's developmental potential as a species? This is the continual decision that lies open to humanity: the freedom to choose its future, and whether this future will be one of harmonious and positive development or not. Without freedom there can be no real love—freedom and love form an integrity in that they belong together. Love as a force of purification can only come into being through freedom. In this regard, the phenomenon of evil is a part of existence and human evolution. All life is continually evolving and so evil, as a phenomenon of evolution, is also changing in how it functions. What we categorise or term as "evil" cannot be viewed as something "outside" or beyond existence for this is not possible. In fact, it may manifest in accordance with each particular stage of evolvement and human development. As a species, we are in need of expanding our perceptual capacities so that we are better able to comprehend how such "unknown phenomena" participate in the human journey—and this includes the phenomenon of evil, negating, or entropic forces. And the more conscious awareness expands, the more it is cognisant of the myriad forces operating in existence that were previously unknown and/or invisible to us. It is the path of balance to attempt to transform forces rather than seek to struggle or push back against them, as this just furthers division and separation and not integration. What is necessary are the capacities of transformation, not the power to destroy: "We can form a quite different relationship to the world if we replace our wish to destroy all forces and energies we judge to be evil with an impulse for their *transformation*."[3] Many philosophers have theorised that evil equates to entanglement in matter. While there is some truth to this perspective, it is only a part of the picture, which overall is more nuanced. For others, the concept of evil represents a limit or threshold to a capacity of perception. We tend to view the fundamentals of negating forces through their manifestations in the physical world yet are unable to perceive the underlying causes or primary impulses. To approach these counterforces, we need to go beyond theory and the arena of our physical senses. By being conscious of the vital forces, we are more able to recognise those aspects, elements, or entities that are in opposition to these vital, energetic forces.

It seems to this author that development and correct evolvement is not an option but an obligation. That is, it is a task that has been given to us to participate in. Yet this necessity for inner development and evolution has been increasingly pushed onto the external world to the detriment of the inner life. The outer, material world accelerates through stages of development (what we often call "progress"), yet the world of spirit is neglected to the point of its near vanishment. Rudolf Steiner refers to this when he said: "This is a most important secret of existence—that the quality integral to our spiritual being, one that represents our highest attainment in the world of spirit, can be wrongly transposed and relocated in the physical realm, so that it becomes our worst aberration."[4] In other words, spiritual attributes that are misplaced in the physical domain can constitute evil. Certain attributes manifested incorrectly, or out of place and time, can bring about negating consequences. And yet there is no "without"—all attributes, essences, and features exist within the realm of our known existence: "If we could not be evil, we could not be spiritual beings either. Without the characteristics which make us evil, we could not enter the spiritual world."[5] Therefore, worldly philosophers who ignore the metaphysical realm are unable to fathom the depths of meaning inherent within the phenomenon of evil. Evil is a phenomenon of our wider reality, and in order to grasp just the tailcoats of this phenomenon we need to have a broader comprehension of reality beyond the limitations of matter-reality. It also helps if a person has a more expansive awareness regarding the "phenomena of the world" above and beyond its programmed precepts. Human reasoning can be used to validate or deny the same event—to uphold contradictions—as was demonstrated by the philosopher Immanuel Kant. Human reason can be critiqued, and therefore so can our hypotheses on truth. If we remain within the confines of reason alone—of the intellect—then we are only as free as the limitations of our thoughts. In other words, we are a prisoner of our own thinking. And yet, in these times especially, a great majority of the human endeavour has been given over to the reasoning power of the intellect. Misplaced intellect can itself act as a counterforce to a balanced and coherent path of development. As mentioned previously, the psychiatrist Iain McGilchrist has said that we are living in a "delusional world" because of the over-dominance of the intellect and left-brain rational thinking. Humanity stands poised on this threshold where intellect and a machinic form of thinking can take us in one direction, whereas imagination, intuition, and a spirit-consciousness can take us in another.

It is the forces of dry, machinic intellect that are currently steering a globalised human society into a future pathway of dark materialism and a nihilism of the soul. This *will to technology* does not navigate its route in accordance with any spiritual or vital forces. On the contrary, it seeks to overtake the will of the human being and to replace this with a framework of automation, certainty, and soul-passivity. There are forces on the Earth, manifesting through what I call the "machinic impulse", that aim to hinder and prevent metaphysical truths and wisdom from entering into the human domain, and they divert these into materialism. A machinic form of technology (for not all technology is necessarily "machinic") coupled with a cognitive programming of materialism leads to a culture of *not-being*. Forces of the material world cannot exert permanent influence over the individual's inner being, yet humanity is being coerced into deadening or hardening the spirit-consciousness within people so that the inner being is silenced into dormancy. One strategy for this deadening is from subliminal and subconscious programming through the media and entertainment culture exerting influence beyond people's conscious awareness. Through the dogma of scientific materialism people have been taught that their thoughts and opinions are their own. That is, thoughts are produced from the act of conscious thinking which is a direct by-product of the neuronal processes of the brain. People are now so materially minded that they believe that "thoughts" spring from their own minds almost as if they were to believe that breathing brings forth oxygen within them rather than being received. What many people are still not aware of is that thoughts can be implanted or directed into the mind of an individual. Also, thoughts and ideas can be picked up from the consciousness field that exists beyond the confines of the physical brain. A person's brain acts as an antenna that decodes information from the collective consciousness field. Furthermore, ideas and opinions can be implanted into an individual through subconscious processes or signals that have been deliberately planted in external forms of information and entertainment. Much of what has been seen as evil is based on falsehood. Negating influences thrive on delusion and illusion, and in a world of deep fakes and "post-truth" these aspects are predominant.

Those forces and impulses opposed to human evolution often attempt to curtail humanity's future by trying to force premature development upon a humanity not yet mature enough to deal with it—such as is the case today with advancing technology and the creation of AI. This aims to block or sabotage the balanced and correct path of human evolution and misdirect it into an alternative direction that ultimately leads not to improvement but implosion or stagnation. Outer, material developments are running ahead of us without a corresponding inner maturity or wisdom being applied. One example of this will be the development of brain chips or human-to-machine interfaces (such as are being developed by Elon Musk's Neuralink company) that will enable new "capacities" and deliver this as a "natural development", yet these abilities will be placed on people without preparing them or people having to make any effort to transform themselves to gain this. Hence, we shall be unprepared and immature. And this will divert or short-change people from having to gain new faculties of communication, or psychic capacities, through a path of organic inner development.

In one sense, humanity is being pushed and compelled to face its immediate "danger of the situation" in order to force through a return to spirit-consciousness. At the same time, these forces are so compelling that people are in danger of succumbing to them. The nihilism and "not-being" that is heavily promoted through tech-materialism is pulling the human vessel further into the heavy calcification of machinic forces. This densification is dulling the instinctive and intuitive senses within the individual, as we are seeing through the skyrocketing apathy, aggression, anger, and antisocial behaviour. The negating forces of automation are bringing into the Earth an energy of rigidity. These forces are pulling individuals back from the threshold and steering them into choices of fear instead of freedom. Oppositional forces create the potentials for making choices as well as offering false opportunities to step back from the path of development.

Oppositional forces of the spiritual dialectic

It is recognised that movement and change are often symbolised through struggle and opposition. In social-historical terms, there have been struggle and opposition between class relations, politics, and more, that have been the cause of varied revolutions where the revolution is often seen to bring about a "resolution". This notion of oppositional struggle to create a third force of resolution is known as a dialectic. That is, the thesis (force) and its antithesis (opposing force) create a synthesis (resolution). The concept of the dialectic struggle was developed by the German philosopher Georg Hegel who wrote that the mind or spirit manifested itself in a set of contradictions and oppositions that were ultimately integrated and united in synthesis. For Hegel, the synthesis (the absolute), must always pass through a stage of opposition in its journey to completion and truth. On a material level, Hegel viewed this dialectic relationship as the process by which human history unfolds. That is, history (social evolution) progresses as a struggle between two opposing forces towards a developmental state of resolution. According to Hegel, the main characteristic of resolution-in-unity was that it evolved through contradiction and denial; or, through struggle with the forces of "evil". These struggles, says Hegel, can be found in most social domains such as history, philosophy, art, nature, and even consciousness. Hegel's thinking was highly influenced by the lesser-known writings of German Christian mystic Jacob Böhme. Böhme's inner visions led him to create a cosmology where it was necessary for humanity to return to God-Source (what he termed the *Urgrund* meaning literally the "original ground" or primary principle). These states of conflict would be a necessary stage in the further completion of the evolution of the universe. Humanity's free will in this separation, conflict, and resolution was the most important gift that God-Source could give to us. In other words, it would be our own responsibility—and a privileged responsibility at that—to work towards our reconciliation through struggle and the opposing forces of resistance.

In a similar manner, the teachings of the Greek-Armenian esoteric philosopher George Gurdjieff also describe a dialectic relationship through the oppositional forces of *Holy Affirming* and *Holy Denying* leading to a *Holy Reconciling*. Gurdjieff referred to this as the "Law of Three". In this context, we can see how a coming together of contradictory impulses—such as mind and spirit or "good and evil"—could lead towards a resolution that would not only be an integration of these contradictory forces but also a resolution/synthesis *greater than* the sum of its parts. Using Gurdjieff's terminology, the Holy Affirming force attracts a Holy Denying force, and this contestation leads to a resolution of the Holy Reconciling—the active, passive, and unifying (also called the neutral). Some astute commentators have recognised dialectical forces operative upon the world stage:

> The practicing "dialecticians" of secret societies and Orders know very well that if one wants to launch into a world-wide adventure on one side, it is necessary to create for oneself a counter-effect from

the other side. Reduced to its simplest terms, this means that as soon as we let the dogs off the leash on one side, the same has to happen on the other; it will not work otherwise. But the one and the other have to be controlled from a unified centre.[6]

In this scenario, the dialectical oppositions are utilised as false opposi-tions to create a situation of controlled chaos that is managed and over-seen by an existing "unified centre". This is exactly the strategy being played out across the global geo-political order today, with the Western unipolar Anglo-American empire of the existing rules-based interna-tional order (RBIO) being falsely pitted against the multi-polar BRICS new world order. While this seems to the uneducated observer to be a contestation of opposing forces, it is actually a false dialectic being controlled from a third force acting as a unified centre. In this context, regarding geo-political events upon the planet, the "third force" is a counter-evolutionary force (an entropic force) that exists as the real, unified negative force. And this negative force is in a dialectical, oppos-ing relationship with the developmental path of human evolution. Within the larger picture, this oppositional "third force" is a hidden hand behind the contesting forces upon the material plane. However, a genuine third force resolution can emerge from within a mingling of opposing forces, just as two metals coming together can form an alloy. Such an approach was described in the Manichean teachings.

The teaching of the prophet Mani—known as *Manichaeism*—pro-poses the two principles of light and dark as essential dualisms. Accord-ing to Mani's teachings, these two dualistic principles work through three epochs. These are: i) Non-interference between light and dark; ii) Interference between both principles and the mingling of light and darkness; and iii) Separation between light and darkness.[7] A distinctive feature of Manichaeism's dualism is in its dynamic aspect—the *min-gling*. These two principles do not remain static or at rest (this static state is only during the first epoch of non-interference); they develop in ever-stronger interaction with one another. This intermingling is what results in matter, which incorporates both aspects of the light and dark. Mani describes this as the darkness devouring the light beings in a kind of metabolic process whereby one substance takes and integrates the other into itself. In this understanding, these dual principles are equal in their status yet opposed to each other in their nature. This means that they occupy equal rank within the participation of the creation process, and matter reality (materiality) is a fusion of the two. Without their participation, interaction, and interplay, no creation is possible. The collaboration of light and dark is what constitutes creation and one aspect does not exist without the other. What this ultimately leads to is the message that both light and darkness are necessary for the creative process. This material world is not the realm of dark forces alone, as certain Gnostic teachings posit, but is formed when light beings/energies become mingled with the darkness. Material existence is an interplay, or collaboration, between the forces/energies of light and darkness, albeit in accordance with their separate natures. And this interaction, which can also be seen as conflict at times, is necessary for the continued evolution within matter-reality.

From the Manichaeism perspective, the light and the darkness are both aspects of creative energies in their own right. And thus, when we engage with the exterior physical world, we are being met with contrasts and polarities. It is these contrasts that create the tangible frictions in life which enable events to unfold and develop. As it is said: nothing grows in a vacuum. If all existence was to be purely "good" then there would be little stimuli to develop or to give opportunities and/or situations where developmental choices would have to be made or rejected. That is, there would be no free will as there would be no concept of choice, freedom, or development, etc. Contrasts, dualisms, and polarities—within the realm of matter-reality—provide the stimuli and frictions necessary for change and momentum. Otherwise, a state of placidity, docility, and/or stagnation would arise. We experience these contrasts through being intermingled together to form the "cauldron of heat"—a combination of light and dark ("good and evil") energies—that form a dynamic of opposition for potential transformation or entrapment. The dynamic is established for evolution or devolution based on the choices made from a place of human free will. The Manichean perspective views existence in the material realm as being a series of stages or periods between a stabilised dynamic of light/dark and periods of imbalance and disruption that cause sudden spurts of growth or decay. When the interaction of opposing forces is stabilised, it can be said that the dualism is momentarily neutralised so that a state of balance is formed where light and dark are in equilibrium. This state is only maintained for a period until the next imbalance emerges that plunges matter-reality into a new excited state of dynamic interaction and the whole cycle repeats itself until a new order of equilibrium and balance is restored. At each cycle of dynamic interaction, contestation, and rebalance, a threshold arises where there is the opportunity for development or decay. It is from a state of expanded perception that this arrangement of duality is perceived and understood as being intrinsic to the whole overarching unity. From a state of lower conscious awareness, it all appears as continual dualistic polarisation. It is the intermingling of light and dark energies that allows for a transfiguration into a new condition or state. In Manichaeism, there is no "punishment" or attacking of evil but rather a utilisation of its forces for transformational purposes. And in this way, it is said in Manichaeism that evil is redeemed because a part of the light enters into evil so that the evil itself is overcome.

Rudolf Steiner also shared the Manichaean perspective in viewing that evil forces have a role to play in creative life and evolution. These counterforces are not foreign or external to processes of evolution but rather are required and are integral to the cosmological system. In this sense, both forces of light/good and dark/evil are eternal properties. As was alluded to earlier, Steiner also refers to evil as an "ill-timed good": "What is evil? Nothing but an ill-timed good ... So we see that evil is nothing else than a mis-placed good."[8] What this also implies is that if actions, choices, and intentions of "good/light" begin to stagnate or turn away (delay) in its path of evolvement, it too can at the wrong moment—the "ill-timing"—turn into darkness. This may be what the techno-materialist path is creating: an alternative to correct evolvement that will create a delay and result in an alignment to the counterforces that eventually results in evil. And those power-hungry controlling forces manipulating the geo-political false dialectics have already made their spiritual decision. And by this, it has been an act of will to oppose the natural forces of human evolution. Their threshold choice shall only take them into a path of eventual stagnation and decay. They are blocked from receiving the vital energies that operate to provide momentum through dynamic oppositional forces. This is because the path of evil only chooses a state of negation with no evolutionary dynamic. Such forces and/or agents have literally cut off their source of evolutionary momentum by adopting a state of containment. As I have described throughout this book, this is a path of not-being and nihilism through submission to the *will to technology* and the techno-materialistic forces. This is, quite literally, a struggle for humanity's soul as it engages in a struggle between spirit and matter.

The Manichaean teaching reveals a process towards the transfiguration of spirit (light) over matter (darkness). The role of the spirit-endowed human being is thus to transform the darkness through the spiritualisation of matter. The inner being of the individual is here guided to overcome (and thus transform) the trappings of materialism and materiality. The continued advancement into a future of techno-tyranny represents a deepening into materialism and the forces of darkness (negating forces). It appears that the continuing drive into techno-materialism will be led by the false "I" or persona/ego of the human being, thus furthering the split from spirit-consciousness. The authentic human being requires freedom, sovereignty, and genuine expression; contrary to this is the automaton—the *robosapiens*. The auto-addict, disempowered, unthinking individual is a "slave to other" and hence a slave to not-being. This is what the darker forces are aiming for in their radical attempt to not only desensitise and dumb down human-ity but also in their intention to strip humans down into a minimal form of existence or a "bare life" (see Chapter Ten). However, in order for developmental potentials within humanity to be activated in full, it is likely that the dark counterforces will first have to push their agenda to the extreme. On this note, Steiner has said: "It is necessary in the great plan that evil, too, should come to a peak ... The good would not be so great a good if it were not to grow through the conquest of evil."[9] The recognition of this situation is what can assist in any future positive transition past what I have termed the "threshold". That is, in understanding that current worldly contestations are an opportunity to activate the "right action" from the inner being of the individual. And this "right action" involves, from my perspective, choices and decisions made from a place of human will in regard to freedom, sovereignty, and spirit-consciousness.

The Manichaean view is that the forces of evil—the negating, counter-evolutionary forces—have been gaining a stronger presence within the inner life of human beings. Yet this can also be regarded as a form of "initiation" for the human individual in terms of recognis-ing these forces within themselves as part of the process of transition-ing past the coming threshold. This dialectic of oppositional forces is not solely a theoretical or intellectual concept but comes alive, along with the knowledge of it, through lived experience. It is out of the lived experience that new opportunities and potentialities emerge. Life is a continual unfolding and developing process. If it becomes static or stagnant then it is in danger of slipping towards a non-evolutionary path where the final state is of dissolution. It may be accurate to say that our current reality is more deeply in the grip of the darker, negating forces, since the material realm is more open to the manifestations of falsehood, deception, and ignorance. Because of this, genuine attempts to provide knowledge and "activations" for increased perception are assaulted by the darker forces operative in the world. And yet, it is these very assaults that provide the opportunity, and impetus, for real developmental work to take place within the human realm. As one commentator stated:

> This period is the greatest opportunity that has existed for many thousands of years for "the Work." Not for thousands of years has there been such a need for people who are able "to work." The reason for this is that the transition from one system to another can come only through the "third force." It cannot come from the passive majority or the active minority, from the governed or the power possessors.[10]

From this viewpoint, the illusive "third force" enables the transition between systems or, in my terminology, past the threshold. Yet it cannot come from within the components of the "passive majority" or the "power possessors", those few in power. Instead, it is a force that acts through the "active minority"—those individuals who are prepared and able to be conduits for the action of spirit-consciousness in matter-reality.

Each individual must decide for themselves how they wish to act in their lifetime. It may be said that a person who is ignorant of such decisions, or who rejects making such a decision, is more likely to fall under the sway of entropic forces, for it is these forces that target (or attract) the unaware or lazy souls. In every sphere of human life—whether social, cultural, or political—there are forces in operation that represent spheres of activity of greater magnitude than most people are able to realise. There are "universal forces" that have been in contention (in motion) for a very long time. As for humanity, all motion, all movement, requires effort. That the many are unaware of this only places more emphasis upon the responsibility of the few who are aware. This has always been the case and is likely to remain so for the time ahead.

* * *

To conclude, the counter-evolutionary forces seek to establish a form or structure of human life on this planet that is devoid of human will as this enables such forces (and their agents) to manipulate human thinking to serve their ends. The aim, I would suggest, is to create a form of intellect or "managed intelligence" to dominate the Earth that is independent of the human mind and spirit-consciousness. For the true human being, this represents a state of nihilism and not-being. And this limited form of intellect would constitute a mass of automated-thinking humans that act as tools of control by these greater forces. The result of this will be a *bare life*—a life stripped of spirit-consciousness and awareness—with the aim of recreating humanity within a sphere of the profane.

Notes

1. Rudolf Steiner, "Evil and the Future of Man" (Lecture GA 185), October 26, 1918, Dornach – https://rsarchive.org/Lectures/19181026p01.html (last accessed 26 May 2025).
2. Rudolf Steiner, *EVIL: Selected Lectures by Rudolf Steiner* (Forest Row, UK: Rudolf Steiner Press, 1997), 178–179.
3. Cited in Rudolf Steiner, *EVIL: Selected Lectures by Rudolf Steiner* (Forest Row, UK: Rudolf Steiner Press, 1997), 11.
4. Rudolf Steiner, *EVIL: Selected Lectures by Rudolf Steiner* (Forest Row, UK: Rudolf Steiner Press, 1997), 30.
5. Rudolf Steiner, *EVIL: Selected Lectures by Rudolf Steiner* (Forest Row, UK: Rudolf Steiner Press, 1997), 30.
6. G. A. Bondarev, *Crisis of Civilization* (London: Wellspring Bookshop, 1993, 2nd Edition), 137.
7. This cosmology is described in the *Cologne Mani Codex*.
8. From a speech Steiner gave on November 11, 1904 (CW 93).
9. Cited in Christine Gruwez, *Mani & Rudolf Steiner* (Great Barrington, MA: SteinerBooks, 2014), 59.
10. Taken from the author's own collected notes (source unknown).

CHAPTER TEN

Bare life (the stripping away of spiritual awareness)

For unto every one that hath shall be given, and he shall have abundance: but from him that hath not shall be taken away even that which he hath
—Matthew 25:29

In the eyes of authority—and maybe rightly so—nothing looks more like a terrorist than the ordinary man
—Giorgio Agamben

Polish psychiatrist Andrzej Łobaczewski, in his book *Political Ponerology*, gave us the study of evil in contemporary politics. Perhaps not surprisingly, Łobaczewski's research had found high percentage levels of psychopathic behaviour within the very top tiers of the political establishment across varied societies. Łobaczewski concluded that if abnormal ways of human behaviour become engrained at the highest levels of our political institutions, then these abnormal modes of behaviour and perspectives are more likely to trickle down and become "normalised" within human cultures. As Łobaczewski says: "If an individual in a position of political power is a psychopath, he or she can create an epidemic of psychopathology in people who are not, essentially, psychopathic."[1] An epidemic of psychopathic thinking is not that hard to create, for thought forms are just as contagious as any biological virus. In fact, they can spread quicker—almost simultaneously. One person can post an idea online, or express an opinion or ideology, and this can be received by other people almost instantaneously at the other end of the world. That is, people across the planet can become "infected" by an idea/opinion/ideology (aka thought form) instantaneously. Through the medium of our technological communications, mass or mob psychology, mental intoxication, and a reprogrammed cultural identity are relatively easy to achieve. According to the now famous clinical psychologist Prof Mattias Desmet, the four sociocultural conditions that allow for easy manipulations of a mass psychology—or an epidemic of psychopathic thinking—to emerge are: a lack of social bonds; people experiencing life as meaningless or senseless; free-floating anxiety; and free-floating frustration and aggression.[2] As previous chapters in this book have explored, there has been a progressive build-up of nihilism, purposelessness, and a sense of not-being, that is now being intensified through the techno-materialistic environment of our lives.

Prof Mattias Desmet believes the world has experienced a huge, global ritual that has established a new form (a recalibrated form) of social bonding. Desmet also states that this newly arrived mass psychology is a manner of compensation for many years of extreme individualism where people felt they now needed to seek out new and different collective bonds of commonality. However, this new arrangement in social allegiances is a socially programmed and managed method of social re-gathering. And it is being accomplished on a worldwide scale through globally implemented strategies of subtle and overt coercion, as well as through agendas of fear and control management. Also, it is brought into being through a form of ritual. Rituals are not only for religious or sacred ceremonies. By definition, and according to the Collins dictionary, a ritual is a ceremony or way of behaving which involves a series of actions performed in a fixed order. And that prescribed or fixed order can come through agreement or imposition—or a mixture of both. Participation in rituals also develops a degree of loyalty to the group/grouping through adherence to and the performing of acts that support the main narratives. These acts of obedience (behaviour sets) can be regarded as rituals, similar to how more familiar religious rituals are performed to denote loyalty to a specific religious faith. When social acts are performed through an emotional attachment of ritual, a form of "hypnotic allegiance" is established that is then extremely hard to break away from. This can then lead to a form of misplaced ethics that can cause people to engage in acts of self-sacrifice in order to uphold what they have been led to believe is their ethical position. People caught up within the mass hypnosis are made to sincerely believe that the mainstream narratives are correct and that they are right to be following and supporting them—even when the evidence points to the contrary. In other words, such people strongly believe in the moral rightness of their position, and this gives them a more powerful sense of solidarity and justification. Similarly, during the religious crusades of the medieval period each side felt they were doing "God's work" by engaging in mass slaughter. What this demonstrates is how easy it is to implement a condition of misplaced ethics.

People swept up within a mass or crowd psychology tend to protect and maintain it whether consciously or unconsciously. This is why they are most likely to reject any contrary information when it is presented to them; or will reject even the chance for such information to be presented. This amounts to a state of mild induced hypnosis which has shifted from an external identification to a self-maintained state. That is, people engage in the process of their own induced hypnosis. Part of the reason for this is that many of the people who accepted the slippage into the formation of a mass psychology were already experiencing psychological discontent. This could come from perceiving a lack of life purpose and meaning; a dislike of their jobs; general restlessness and anxiety; and similar issues related to their previous life status. Many people caught within the mass programming believe themselves to be expressing their own opinions when in fact there has been a clever sleight of hand in that they have been provided with a set of preformed "opinion bundles" that they can then put forward as their own. Such people are often expressing what they believe to be personal opinions yet not arrived at through individual perceptive awareness or critical questioning but rather conditioned "thought bundles" provided through the programming techniques built into the establishment of the psychological collective mass. That is, mass hypnosis comes with a pre-prepared collection of opinion sets for bulk dispersal. These are all strategies carefully concealed with the "apparatus" of power.

The Apparatus

The term "apparatus" in the context used here is a particular designation that refers to the technology of power. It was used in a specific way by French social theorist Michel Foucault, who defined it as:

> ... the nature of an apparatus is essentially strategic, which means that we are speaking about a certain manipulation of relations of forces, of a rational and concrete intervention in the relations of forces, either so as to develop them in a particular direction, or to block them, to stabilize them, and to utilise them. The apparatus is thus always inscribed into a play of power, but it is also always linked to certain limits of knowledge that arise from it and, to an equal degree, condition it. The apparatus is precisely this: a set of strategies of the relations of forces supporting, and supported by, certain types of knowledge.[3]

As Foucault states, it is the strategic forces of power supported by specific knowledge. In these current times, this knowledge is highly technological and aligned with deep occult understanding of the metaphysical or unseen realms operative within this dimension of existence. Further, the Apparatus (as I now refer to it) is a deeply pervasive network that has been established between the technologies that create power and those networks that sustain these power relations. These Apparatuses or technologies of power are both material (physical) and immaterial (digital) and must, by their necessity, produce their "subject" (e.g., the human being) within their mechanised (and increasingly automated) arrangements of social control. The Italian philosopher Giorgio Agamben has more recently expanded upon Foucault's notion of the "apparatus" to define it: "I shall call an apparatus literally anything that has in some way the capacity to capture, orient, determine, intercept, model, control, or secure the gestures, behaviors, opinions, or discourses of living beings."[4] Agamben states clearly that in his opinion of this Apparatus of power relations, there are two major classes, which are the living beings and apparatuses. And that between these two, as a third class, there are the "subjects" that result from the continual struggle between living beings and Apparatuses. The more subjects (i.e., humans) that are available for subjectification, then the greater the growth of Apparatuses and their entwined technologies of power: "We could say that today there is not even a single instant in which the life of individuals is not modeled, contaminated, or controlled by some apparatus."[5] And this environment of contamination and control marks the energetic, vibratory realm of the negating path—the path of rejection and denial of the genuine human being and its purpose on this planet. The instruments of this denial are the gadgets and devices, the software and the algorithms, that are all surreptitiously programmed into a network, an Apparatus, of social management that captures not only the physical vessel of the human being but also its soul—our very *being-ness*. Through the increasing not-being of human behaviour and human relations arises the power of a profane life that diminishes the sanctity of spirit-consciousness (see Chapter Eleven for more on the profane life). In short, the path of denial of spirit is one that profanes the human being.

Modern forms of power have been furtively embedded within the fabric of our societies through Apparatuses that are now predominantly technologically composed. This road to continued segregation and categorisation is contrary to the sacredness of life; in fact, it constitutes the path of anti-life (in the organic sense, at least). Such profanity is the very negation of the human being into a condition of "not-being". It is no doubt for this reason, the encroaching profanity of our contemporary societies, which is responsible for producing a widespread sense of subjectification and loss of purpose within so many individuals. What the current epoch is witnessing as it approaches its threshold (of collapse or recalibration) is a rampant agenda of dehumanisation upon a scale hitherto unseen. And if global humanity remains on this path—the path of denial—then it is facing imminent catastrophe. The bio-techno-political machine within the Apparatus has driven more and more human societies into a *state of exception*. Giorgio Agamben, whose book *State of Exception* (2005) examined this phenomenon, concurs that the state of exception, which has a biopolitical significance, is also an Apparatus of power that can now be wielded through a technological framework or architecture. How can the "state of exception" be defined? This is a murky area, and Agamben also notes the difficulty of definition here, for the state of exception is also closely related to civil war, insurrection, and resistance in its connection to a state of emergency.[6] Due in large part to the undemocratic practices of contemporary nation states, the crossing of lawful and judicial thresholds has established a blurred domain where the absence of civil rights meshes with the rise of civil unrest.

As such, many modern states now seem to be in a "permanent state of emergency" where the exception has become the rule. Agamben concludes that "... the state of exception tends increasingly to appear as the dominant paradigm of government in contemporary politics."[7] And the dominant paradigm currently utilised by technocratic authorities is the state of emergency (or the "state of siege") which gives these ruling powers an expansion of executive powers. The state of emergency is usually declared during hostilities and internal civil unrest, which then gives a further excuse for expanding non-democratic executive powers. This is the Hegelian dialectic of creating the problem in order to elicit a reaction so as to enforce a solution.

Such states of exception have also historically been viewed through the figure of dictatorship, which now has been transmuted into modern forms of technocracy. The political theorist Carl Schmitt argued that dictatorship is not an aberration or an exception in the history of politics but rather an essential and legitimate form of government that is necessary in times of crisis. Schmitt contends that the modern state, which is allegedly based on the rule of law, is ill-equipped to deal with extraordinary circumstances such as arise during hostilities; and more so when such hostilities and crises are asymmetrical and may include contributing factors such as a dissolving civil society and economic collapse. In these situations, the state persuades itself, and its citizens, that it must be able to act "decisively and quickly", without the constraints of normal legal procedures. Hence, the creation of a state of exception allows for a theatre of operations that is devoid of law and where the distinction between public and private are intentionally dissolved. Legality is not required to create new laws—only the *power to create laws* is necessary. This leaves a dangerous space, and sets a hazardous precedent, where the Apparatus shifts up a gear and further distances life (the act of living) from the sanctity of life, and existence is further split from a sacred source. The end result is a "bare life", which is the product of the technocratic machine, and where to be alive is not the same thing as living, or "life" as we understand it. In essence, all material forms are alive—but not all material forms are living. Biological life is not the same distinction as conscious life. There is a different order of *organisation* present in these distinct forms.

Contemporary life has now come under the jurisdiction of a technologised global Apparatus that regards "biological life" as a state to be regulated within its framework. This is because once biological life (bio-life) is registered within the framework of a trans-national body of power, then it can be included within its remit of governance. Bio-life then gets interpreted as bio-power. And to uphold the authority of bio-power, biological life has to become subjectivised and thus transformed into weak or *docile bodies*.[8] This stripped-down representation of biological life is what Giorgio Agamben refers to as *bare life*. While Agamben considers "bare life" from a political perspective, I would view it from a metaphysical angle; that is, as a physical, biological construct that has been stripped of its spiritual and sacred aspects. The sovereign human individual is thus modified into a machinic construct; a set of data that can be uploaded into the AI-fuelled Apparatus of occult, techno-materialistic power. The "bare life" establishes human life through the "datafied" framework that targets the very constituents of the human condition. These are forms of subjectification of the individual based on "identities"—social, political, and sexual. These identities are linked to external doctrines of power that have become increasingly indistinct. We can now see how our current global civilisation has been hijacked from above (above national governance) and mutated into an amorphous state of exception. Meta-power over the individual is now shapeless, fluid, and vague, so that it cannot be clearly seen from the micro-position despite it being duly enforced from the macro-position.

Biological life has been subjectivised as a "bare life" so that it becomes easier to merge into a centralised technological Apparatus of power. By this, human life is subsumed into a machinic framework that then translates it into a transhumanist agenda. This is the present and future agenda that has sought to mould and shape the formless collective masses into a homogenous psychological gel that can be manipulated and bent into conformity and obedience by unseen power structures. According to Agamben, the human being that is "bare life" can be killed but not sacrificed. In this, the body can be suppressed and "evicted" from participation in the world, yet cannot be praised, celebrated, or ritualised in any way. In all aspects, the human being is stripped of sacred recognition, and thus cannot be "sacrificed" for this denotes a sacred ritual or at least one of homage.[9] Conscious life—and especially an interiorised, spiritualised life—is an abomination for the bare life of technocratic tyranny where the AI god is close at hand. The organic sacred, a realm where the biological body and spirit-consciousness are in correspondence with cosmic forces and psychic powers, is regarded as the number one threat to the Apparatus of bare life. People are at "liberty" to revolt, to a specified degree and within boundaries, yet they are not given liberty to be spirituality activated sovereign individuals whose allegiance is to a sacred intelligence beyond the techno-material forms of power. The human individual is effectively a *not-being* within a *docile* body, devoid of social distinction. Within the unfolding path of denial, any person born within a physical location will become a data-body under the jurisdiction of a technocratic Apparatus. No one is granted immunity unless they succumb to the new rules that are, by contrast, established to create conformity to the dominant program. The only true immunity available within this profane realm is through a sacred path and sacred acts. The real threat to this civilisation of denial and negation is through the metaphysical or spiritualised gateway— the path of *sacred taboo*—where awakening to greater perception and expanded awareness is the greatest crime.

* * *

The "bare life" of not-being that has been explored within the chapters of this book demonstrates a potential pathway into a future that will become even more anti-human than at present. It is a path of denial of the human spirit—of the soul within humanity—and a subjugation (willing or not) to forces beyond the human that do not have our interests at heart. On the contrary, these forces of technocratic power aim to mute and transmute the human individual into a form of *golem*—a lifeless and automated data-body that is dependent upon an external body, or "master", that wields ultimate authority. It is a pathway into density and darkness, away from the natural light of evolvement and growth. The realm of greatest density is that place furthest removed from the light of the sun. The absence of light is the true realm of darkness. This is why hell is often depicted as being in the subterranean realm—the *underworld*—beneath the earth where the mineralisation is denser. This is the realm of hard rock, whose time of existence stretches over millions, or even billions, of years. Density, mineralisation, heaviness: these were also the themes depicted by Dante in his description of Inferno.

Dante's journey in the interior of the Earth consisted of concentric circles of ever-increasing density. Similarly, the machinic architecture of a tech-materialistic world is dependent on the mineralisation of silicon at its core. And its virtual worlds and metaverses, through goggles and headsets, produce a blindness to the natural light of the physical world and thus further removes the individual from the light of our star-sun. The only places in the physical world where sunlight does not penetrate are situated in the mineral interior—in the caverns, tunnels, and mines—where the darkness seems to diminish our capacity for happiness: "Light is evidently in some way *food* for the emotional side of man, and we can only take the idea of his consignment to a lightless hell to symbolise the fact that this side of him has *already died*."[10] The old interior of the Earth is now being replaced by the machinic reproductions of our digital-virtual worlds where human eyes are blinded not by layers of earth but the technological apparatuses strapped over our faces. Here, in the digital realm, avatars live forever, and time has no meaning. In our ancient descriptions of hell, all these three ideas are combined: the subterranean or interior realm; the darkness or absence of natural light; and the everlasting or immensely long sense of time duration. This is the Babylonian myth of Aralu, the "land of no return", the region of darkness where the inhabitants see no natural light. And yet the presence of a "Hell" is a warning to us. It is a realm of stagnation; a realm where time cannot renew itself, for it is slowed down into an immensely long stretch of linear time: time with no end. This is a profanity. It is a life without potential for change, for beginning again. Whereas the sacred has always been about the opportunity for rejuvenation and starting again, the profane realm replaces essence with form; being with not-being; integration with disintegration; unity with fragmentation. The technocratic future—the path of denial—is seeking to calculate and categorise everything. It aims not only to measure time but to dictate it, and to control it. This is an act of profanity within a cosmic sacred order. History cannot be fixed into place, crystallised, for the catastrophe may be just as important for human life as its period of renewal. As we shall see, true history may actually exist out of time.

Notes

1. Andrew Łobaczewski, *Political Ponerology: A Science on the Nature of Evil Adjusted for Political Purposes* (Otto, NC: Red Pill Press, 2007).
2. Mattias Desmet, *The Psychology of Totalitarianism* (White River Junction, VT: Chelsea Green Publishing Co, 2022).
3. Cited in Giorgio Agamben, *What Is an Apparatus & Other Essays* (Redwood City, CA: Stanford University Press, 2009), 2.

4. Giorgio Agamben, *What Is an Apparatus & Other Essays* (Redwood City, CA: Stanford University Press, 2009), 14.

5. Giorgio Agamben, *What Is an Apparatus & Other Essays* (Redwood City, CA: Stanford University Press, 2009), 15.

6. Giorgio Agamben, *State of Exception* (Chicago, IL: Chicago University Press, 2005).

7. Giorgio Agamben, *State of Exception* (Chicago, IL: Chicago University Press, 2005), 2.

8. The term "docile bodies" was explored in the work of French philosopher Michel Foucault, especially in his book *Discipline and Punish* (London: Vintage, 1975).

9. Giorgio Agamben, *Homo Sacer: Sovereign Power and Bare Life* (Redwood City, CA: Stanford University Press, 1998).

10. Rodney Collin, *The Theory of Eternal Life* (London: Vincent Stuart Publishers, 1956), 63.

CHAPTER ELEVEN

Profane society (the dark night of civilisation)

I believe that if history is to be meaningful its meaning must originate outside of itself—in other words, outside of time and space

—Kyriacos C. Markides

Modern society is intensely secular; even those who regret this admit it. The irony is that, after excluding the mystical tradition from our cultural mainstream and claiming to find it irrelevant to our concerns, so many others feel empty without it

—David Maybury-Lewis

Contrary to the populist view of society as an exemplar of linear progression, life on this planet has gone through cycles and cyclic patterns of development and decay, which can also be seen through the lens of catastrophe and renewal. Short-sightedness is linear, which may explain why the average eighty-year span of a human life appears as a linear progression. Long-term patterns, however, are more likely to ebb and flow along with the fluctuation of the cosmic winds. In the modern era, the secular-materialist view of linear progress has taken dominance. Yet this view has prevailed for only a relatively short time in contrast to much older perceptions of how time manifests upon this Earth. From earliest

written records, philosophers have perceived the rise and fall of civilisations upon the planet like the in-flow and out-flow of breath. The most
well-known in the Western hemisphere are the views inherited from the
Ancient Greeks; the rise and fall of civilisations in cycles like the sea-
sons was put forth by Plato (428–348 BC) and Aristotle (384–322 BC) and
polished further by Polybius (200–118 BC). In Polybius's *Anacyclosis*,
the political pattern of cycles follows the sequence of monarchy, king-
ship, tyranny, aristocracy, oligarchy, democracy, and ochlocracy before a
period of barbarianism resets the cycle. Even earlier than this, the Greek
poet and thinker Hesiod had put forth the cycle of the four ages—Gold,
Silver, Bronze, and Iron—which has correspondences to the cyclic ages
of the Zoroastrians and the Hindu Yuga cycles. These cycles, as depicted
by the quality of metal, depict a rotational movement between epochs
of splendour and achievement interspersed with ages of degeneration
and decay. Later, the Christian religious model posited an almost fated
cycle of judgement, retribution, and restoration that is bookended by
the Book of Revelation, (also known as the Apocalypse of John). In a
similar manner, the "living organism" model has been supported by
thinkers throughout recorded history where birth, death, and rebirth
feed into a recurring incarnational cycle. The great Arab historian and
philosopher Ibn Khaldun (1332–1406) described a cyclic movement of
accumulated knowledge with each new civilisation growing out of the
ashes of the preceding one.

As many cultural historians have noted, large-scale violence and
disruption usually erupt at the end of a cyclic age or epoch. Bibhu Dev
Misra, a researcher into Indian history, notes how people generally lose
their sanity at the end of a Yuga cycle:

> The two Indian epics, the Ramayana and the Mahabharata,
> describe the fierce battles that were fought during the periods of
> transition from the Treta Yuga to the Dwapara Yuga and from the
> Dwapara Yuga to the Kali Yuga respectively. The Greek epic Iliad,
> on the other hand, provides an account of the Trojan War which
> was fought during the period of transition between the descending
> and the ascending Kali Yuga.[1]

Misra goes on to suggest that the grand cyclic transitions between
Yugas, which take place over years, even decades, create an alteration
in the energy balance upon the planet that causes whole regions and

multitudes of people to lose their sanity. One hypothesis that fits in here is that the current rise of a global technocratic tyranny represents the dark energy of an ending age. In the midst of such transitions many people will be losing their heads (quite literally), while there will be others who align themselves with the subtle incoming energies that represent the new unfolding epoch that, like the early seeds, is sprouting up from the scorched earth. The extremity and excesses that mark the end of an age give rise to visible profanities within our societies and cultures. These profanities may be the breakdown in ethics, morality, the fragmentation in social identities, and all manner of distasteful cultural eruptions. These scenes can be taken to represent the "hell on earth" that has symbolically existed to assist in humanity's restoration to the sacred at the appointed time. According to philosopher Rodney Collin: "The purpose of hell, then, would be to restore faulty psychic products to their original state of sound raw material, which in due course could be used again, that is, re-absorbed into growing forms."[2]

The moral and ethical descent into hell signifies a journey that initially portrays a countermovement in evolvement and development, such as can be represented by the transhumanist technocracy. It is a temporary falling back into a lesser state—the path of denial—that, at some point, acts as a trigger to activate once more a rising movement upon the cyclic wheel of civilisational change. The immersion into profanity acts as a temporary period of stagnation that simultaneously functions as a state of awareness, through absence, of the need for a sacred connection once again. As Collin states, the purpose of hell is to restore the fault in the psychic state of humanity; and this pre-empts not a social revolution by fire but a psychic revolution through expanded conscious awareness. What I refer to here is about getting back on the right path. If the human being, individually and collectively, continues to live under conditions that are contrary to their innate nature and basic requirements for a healthy and sane life then at some point, if civilisation is not to perish, conditions will need to be readjusted in correspondence to the new needs of the human being. As psychoanalyst Erich Fromm noted, "The fact that millions of people share the same mental pathology does not make these people sane."[3] History in any given regional environment is a shared dominant narrative that provides a framework of meaning that largely goes unquestioned. Yet, as Markides says in the opening citation, meaning must originate outside history; that is, the physical aspect is to be receptive and open to what can come into the material realm to infuse it with purpose. The profane is the closing down to those influences it deems unfamiliar and to restrict awareness upon the physical plane. And the sacred influences are those that originate from outside the reality construct yet are able to penetrate the veil through various means (such as through the religious-spiritual or paranormal).

The French mystic-philosopher Rene Guenon wrote several books warning that increased materialism and physical trappings will lead to a "solidification of the world" resulting in "fissures" opening up through which "infra-psychic" forces can enter. In the conclusion of his book *The Reign of Quantity*, Rene Guenon wrote: "So it is that if one wishes to penetrate to the deepest level of reality, one can say in all objective truth that 'the end of the world' is never and can never be anything but the end of an illusion."[4] And where the sacred distinguishes, the profane divides. The human order and the cosmic order are not, in reality, separated; they are only considered to be so by a modern profane perspective. The sacred perspective recognises that the cosmic and human order are in continual correspondence and are also bound by related events and influences, such as is related by the cyclic models. It is recognised that there is no break in the correspondence between the cosmic and the human order, and that cataclysmic events on Earth often fall into this periodic correspondence. Guenon states that materiality as an end in itself is inherently an unrealisable condition. This is because it replaces the sacred with an "inertness". It breaks down the organic relationship between the cosmic and the human realms; it dismisses the relationality of influences and therefore seeks to "play god" through matter-reality alone. This is why those of the transhumanist path feel justified to create AI gods as a substitution for the sacred, for they consider these deities as based on a quantitative level of intelligence rather than a cosmic mandate. This is the negated or Lesser Reality discussed previously (see Chapter Five) where only that which is tangible is real. The "will to technology" can be consecrated as there is no sacred backdrop (no metaphysical background) in which to contest this, according to the deep materialism of a technocratic modernity. The techno-theological path is a closed system; it encases life within its own vacuum shell and denies the interpenetration of cosmic and sacred influences. And a closed system must eventually come to its own demise through entropy, for no new energy is coming into the system to renew it. Techno-materialism must therefore inevitably result in a sociocultural breakdown and eventual demise.

Life provides events, encounters, and crises where choices are to be made by both the individual human being as well as the collective. Yet such choices and decisions can only be fully made if they are embedded within a comprehension of a transcendental, metaphysical reality. The longer the human being is kept isolated from such a transcendental, metaphysical reality then the more likely it will be that their perceptive, intuitive, and clairvoyant faculties will atrophy. And it may very well be that the atrophy of such faculties is what lies at the heart of the technocratic agenda. The organic evolutionary trajectory is undergoing sabotage and is being hijacked into a transhumanist future pathway. As mentioned previously, such a future pathway would turn into an evolutionary cul-de-sac or dead end—at least where organic, biological human beings are concerned. Artificial modifications do not take into account the correspondence to a cosmic, sacred order. As such, they are implemented almost blindly and lead to a de-harmonisation and disequilibrium in the corresponding order. What is presented to us in its place is a "counterpart"—a replicant or substituted reality—like having a person replaced by a clone. Organic life effectively is being cloned into a techno-materialistic one. Because of full immersion into the counterpart or counterfeit world, the human being loses perception and recognition of the interpenetrating metaphysical impulses. Rene Guenon fully recognised this when he wrote more than three-quarters of a century ago:

> ... because of what has just been called its "counterpart" he loses in addition all chance of becoming aware of a manifest intervention of supra-sensible elements in the sensible world itself. So for him the world has become to the greatest possible extent completely "closed," for it has become ever more "solid" as it has become more isolated from every other order of reality ...[5]

This increased solidification must inevitably lead, as already noted by Guenon, to "fissures" or cracks appearing whereby "supra-sensible" elements (influences from the sacred) will noticeably enter. This is because the human and cosmic order must be kept in correspondence at all times; and if an artificial bubble is placed around the human realm, then the sacred order will push against this even more strongly. And this pushing will create more noticeable manifestations— or interpenetrations—whereas previously this interplay was more of a natural and unhindered flow. And it may well be that it is these "forced interpenetrations" that create visible or recognised disturbances within the human realm.

The necessity to remain in correspondence with the sacred order was well known to ancient philosophies and traditions. In the Hindu tradition, for example, a spiritual discipline was established to keep a person within the sacred domain of life. The path of Advaita Vedanta outlines four qualifications to complete the stages. They are, in brief, i) the possession of the natural ability to discern between reality and illusion; in other words, discrimination (*viveka*); ii) readiness to give up all sensuous pleasures and distractions and to become indifferent to them (*vairagya*); iii) the practice of mental tranquillity, self-control, dispassion, endurance, concentration, and faith (*satsampat*); and iv) right desire; that is, the desire for internal attainment above all external things (*mumuksatva*). These qualifications assist in the three stages of hearing (*sravan*); discriminating understanding (*manana*); and constant meditation and awareness (*nididhyasana*). These are all qualities and aspects aimed at developing and sustaining a natural ability to discern between reality and illusion, and to maintain the sacred correspondence within a profane world. Also noteworthy is the Sanskrit word/notion of *pralaya* that refers to an end times state of destruction; or rather, dissolution at the end of a cycle that is followed by a reabsorption and the start of a fresh cycle. It likewise corresponds to a transcendental phase of consciousness whereby perceptual cognition is transformed in order to be appropriate for the beginning of a new cycle. The American monk Thomas Merton, in referring to Hindu religious thought, commented that:

> The Gita [*Bhagavad Gita*] brings to the West a salutary reminder that our highly activistic and one-sided culture is faced with a crisis that may end in self-destruction because it lacks the inner depth of an authentic metaphysical consciousness ... it is because of an inner split and self-alienation which have characterized the Western mind in its single-minded dedication to only half of life: that which is exterior, objective and quantitative.[6]

Metaphysically, beginnings and endings may be illusory; yet physically, they are significant (and symbolic) markers of a timeless realm within which human time is manifested. Within a profane world, many are blind to the offerings from a state of sacred understanding. The modern person trusts more the words of the scientist, the newsreader, the politician, or even the so-called "expert" than they do those words that either originate from the sacred traditions or the subtle words of a modern-day metaphysician.

Between the sacred and the profane, of time eternal and temporal, the human being stands as the bridge of this union. And the current period in human history may well represent the threshold to a time of restoration. That is, a certain restoration of cosmic harmony is needed in order to remain aligned with the pulses of cosmic evolutionary time. In alchemical terms, this is the process of *solve et coagula*: first, the primal matter is to be dissolved (separated into its constituent parts) before then being "worked upon" to be reassembled (coagulated) into a new arrangement. This process has also been symbolised as a form of death and rebirth for the individual; also interpreted as "to die before you die". Once the symbolic nature of the phenomenal world has been understood, the practical steps to be taken will then become evident for the individual, each according to their life context and circumstances. According to Robin Waterfield:

> This process in its general aspect can be described as the re-sacralization of the universe, the restoration of meaning to life in all its aspects and activities, above and beyond scientific materialism and practical utility. This re-sacralization can and should begin with the simplest and the most mundane aspects of our lives on a daily basis: awakening from sleep as a resurrection from death and darkness ...[7]

Given the restoration of human longing for connection with something "beyond" its current limited worldview and perception—a connection with the cosmic or sacred order—then this suggests the need for a process of initiation. The greatest symbols of initiation are birth and death; and these are the exact same processes, both literal and metaphorical, that the world is going through right now. This micro process also may correspond to a macro initiation on a collective level. Any initiation encounter is thus likely to place us face to face with the darker, mortal aspects of our existence: with death, disruption, chaos, and a crisis of community and civilisation. That we have no cultural memory of having encountered such an epochal transition before places us in frightening new territory. As Richard Tarnas states:

> Perhaps the fact that our culture does not provide rituals of initiation is not simply a massive cultural error, but rather reflects and even impels the immersion of the entire culture in its own massive collective initiation. Perhaps we, as a civilization and a species, are undergoing a rite of passage of the most epochal and profound kind, acted out on the stage of history with, as it were, the cosmos itself as the tribal matrix of the initiatory drama.[8]

Tarnas goes on to say that as a species we may now be engaged in a race between initiation and catastrophe. At the same time, however, we do not fully understand the process of initiation—of having to face our dark side, pass through a series of struggles, and emerge the hero.

Part of the initiation—the suffering and the inner/outer struggles—is an intrinsic search for meaning; the journey to the underworld and back is not only an external test of fortitude, willpower, and determination, it is also a necessary journey to purge and prepare. The ordeal sets us up to emerge after the trial as a matured and, hopefully, wiser being. The collective consciousness of humanity is currently manifesting tremors that are all too often manipulated by social forces into fear and insecurity. Yet we are required to transform our species mind, our collective thinking, into a more energised, focused, and integral mind-at-large. We are teetering on the edge of the hero's journey—the descent into the underworld and back—that is the initiation, the rite of passage, our dark night of the soul.[9] The "dark night of the soul" may involve a personal and collective crisis of meaning, a disorientation (perhaps even despair) where identity of the self is dissolved and renewed. This process has often been depicted in myth as a rite of passage. According to famed mythologist Joseph Campbell, there are three phases in the rites of passage: separation, initiation, and return. The middle phase of initiation is the transformative stage, the transitional impulse and transfiguration that sets up the way forward for the return: a return to the world as a renewed force. Initiation is both personal and social. It provides for the inner growth of the individual as well as liberation from illusions—and sociocultural liberation from outworn myths and delusions. Yet the pivotal and operative notion in the hero's journey is that after the initiatory event, the return is accomplished. On the part of the individual, this means a return to one's community, culture, or society, so that the benefits of the transformation can be shared with others. If there is no return, the journey is incomplete. Most human societies lack any form of initiation, whether it be as a sacred form or as an entry path into a craft or association. Where such forms do exist, they are profaned. The profusion of gangs and gang violence across the world, with such gangs having their specific "codes of honour" and rites, shows how deeply such once sacred forms have regressed into their profane aspects. And this profusion of profane mimicry and parody is one indication of how humanity has entered a critical time or crisis period—it's "dark night of civilisation".

Our own civilisational "dark night of the soul" may very well symbolise humanity's own death–rebirth ritual that shamanistic and indigenous cultures recognise during transitions, such as from childhood to adulthood; from dependence to independence; from innocence to maturity. By passing through a global initiation period, experienced as a mass psychical immersion, we may be provided with the energies and impulses to catalyse a growth in psychical awareness and understanding. This could also symbolise a transition from a mental/intellect stage to an integral stage of consciousness. A shared psychological trauma combined with a series of profound physical crises may be the necessary requirements—the minimum price of admission—for the global initiatory immersion towards a psychophysical transformation of human life on planet Earth. Without any such transformation, life on this planet would only dive deeper and faster into the abyss of secular techno-materialism and almost complete separation and alienation from sacred influences. In other words, a complete immersion into a global technocracy.

Within our incumbent institutions, the sacred and the metaphysical are mocked and callously misrepresented through orthodox structures and dogmas that bear no resemblance to the original aspects of truth-consciousness. As David Maybury-Lewis pointed out in the opening citation, people may claim that the sacred is irrelevant to our modern concerns, yet they are also feeling empty without it. This may be because without such *presence* there is a lack of a sense of *being*—what I have repeatedly referred to as a state of *not-being*. As famed anthropologist Claude Levi-Strauss pronounced: "… the *sacred* is equivalent to a *power*, and, in the last analysis, to *reality*. The sacred is saturated with *being*."[10]

The so-called modern techno-materialist mindset views the physical world as a closed system, which establishes this realm as increasingly profane as it sees it as separate from a sacred context. And yet what was once referred to as the "savage mind" has shown an almost mystical understanding of how the sacred informs the very order of universal reality. According to the work of anthropologists Levi-Strauss, Mircea Eliade, and others, the essential nature of primeval or authentic life is that which also sets up a correspondence with the primordial, sacred wisdom. In relation to this, materialistic thinking appears to bear the hallmarks of a stone-cold laboratory. This laboratory ages with time (a profane characteristic), whereas the sacred truths are timeless, yet only dress in the periodic rags of time. To paraphrase the philosopher Huston Smith, trying to live within the profane world would be like living in a house's scaffolding; and to love the transient nature of profane, material things is like embracing your lover's skeleton in place of their soul. And like the body's material skeleton and its immaterial soul, the profane and the sacred exist together as aspects of existence, with the noticeable difference that the sacred infuses the profane and not the other way around. Similarly, the supraconscious can dwell within both the conscious and the unconscious mind; yet these lower minds are unable to flow into the higher. For here, the higher infuses the lower and helps it to raise its awareness, although the lower is unable to infuse that which is higher—just as water runs downhill and not upwards. The sacred influences are needed to infuse the lower, materialistic realm in order to prepare the mental, psychic environment for expanded perceptions. Such forces may appear destructive during the transmutation stage, yet they are necessary to deconstruct the pre-existing reality construct that has been held together by the denser, material energies. These lower vibratory realms have to be dismantled in order for a new phase of civilisational growth.

The Tower of Babel can be said to have represented the profane approach of trying to reach into the heavens—the sacred order—from a materialistic position. The tower was struck down, similar to the lightning-struck tower of the Tarot deck, which is associated with destructive forces, sudden change, and a potentially disruptive revelation that allows for transformation. The destruction of such towers symbolises penetration of the dark world's fire—the dismantling of hubris and materialistic thought—so that purification and revelation shall appear. For some, this may represent or symbolise the end times. For others, the crossing of a threshold.

Notes

1. Bibhu Dev Misra, *Yuga Shift: The End of the Kali Yuga & The Impending Planetary Transformation* (Ajitgarh, India: White Falcon Publishing, 2023), 360.

2. Rodney Collin, *The Theory of Eternal Life* (London: Vincent Stuart Publishers, 1956), 64.

3. Erich Fromm, *The Sane Society* (London: Routledge, 1956/2002), 15.

4. Rene Guenon, *The Reign of Quantity and the Signs of the Times* (Hillsdale, NY: Sophia Perennis, 2004b).

5. Rene Guenon, *The Reign of Quantity and the Signs of the Times* (Hillsdale, NY: Sophia Perennis, 2004b), 146.

6. Cited in Robin Waterfield, *Rene Guenon and the Future of the West: The Life and Writings of a 20th-Century Metaphysician* (Hillsdale, NY: Sophia Perennis, 2017), 89–90.

7. Robin Waterfield, *Rene Guenon and the Future of the West: The Life and Writings of a 20th-Century Metaphysician* (Hillsdale, NY: Sophia Perennis, 2017), 111.

8. Richard Tarnas, "Is the Modern Psyche Undergoing a Rite of Passage?", http://cosmosandpsyche.com/Essays.php (2001), 19.

9. *Dark Night of the Soul* is the title of a poem and treatise written by sixteenth-century Spanish Roman Catholic mystic Saint John of the Cross.

10. Cited in Huston Smith, *Forgotten Truth: The Common Vision of the World's Religions* (New York: HarperCollins, 1992), 3.

CHAPTER TWELVE

Dark world's fire (purification and revelation)

> But, indeed, the shadows are lengthening; the voices of insanity are
> becoming louder. We are in reach of achieving a state of humanity
> which corresponds to the vision of our great teachers; yet we are in
> danger of the destruction of all civilization, or of robotization.
>
> The new phase of human history, if it comes to pass, will be a new
> beginning, not an end
>
> —Erich Fromm

The above opening two quotes from psychoanalyst Erich Fromm are
taken from the conclusion of his work *The Sane Society*, first published
in 1955. Almost three-quarters of a century ago, Fromm perceived the
looming dangers of civilisational destruction, rationalised (in)sanity,
and potential "robotization". He also foresaw that this situation could
be indicative of the demise of a present phase of human history and the
emergence of a new one. And this new phase would mark a beginning,
not an end. It is usually the "end of things" that catches our attention
more than the signs of a new birth. We are shocked at the devastation
of scorched earth yet fail to see the nutrient-rich soil providing for the

sprouting of new seedlings. We are a species hardwired into survival fear, with that fear conditioned to react to short-term danger rather than perceiving the promises of a long-term future. All things come to pass in one way or another. Or to put it another way: this too shall pass.

Life is not a linear process. As discussed in the previous chapter, patterns of change upon the Earth are more likely to be cyclic. Beginnings and endings merge one into another; transitions are the in-between periods that prepare life for crossing a threshold (or for a threshold collapse). To some degree, humanity acts as an automaton existing within a world of machines. An individual reacts to stimuli that they may not consciously be aware of; their thoughts are borrowed from the sea of culture that they swim within—or they may be implanted directly into their thought processes. On another level, a human being is capable of genuine freedom. Both worlds are open to the individual, yet only one path is ultimately chosen. The question may lie in how a person is able to transform the energies and circumstances of their life. It is written in the New Testament: "The axe is already at the root of the trees, and every tree that does not produce good fruit will be cut down and thrown into the fire" (Mathew 3:10). The most basic purpose of the tree is as energy (firewood), and yet the tree is capable of so much more (producing good fruit). The tree can achieve a more significant purpose to its life; yet if it does not do so, then it shall be utilised (cut down) for its primary property (energy). Transformation is an endemic requirement to life on this planet. According to philosopher J. G. Bennett: "Transformation is a task which we have to accomplish together, and those who can do more have to help those who can do less. To be able to do more is to have an obligation, not only to oneself but towards others."[1] It is not outward power that accomplishes great deeds, but the power of inner strength. It is this subtle yet powerful capacity that is tested during the interval periods of transition. Within the Hindu scripture of the Bhagavad Gita there is only one phrase that appears twice—"*Sreyan svadharmo vigunah panadharmat svanustitat*" (Bhagavad Gita 3: 35)—which says, it is better to follow one's own destiny, even if it is without merit, than to follow the destiny of another, however well it may be accomplished. The conditions and circumstances that exist for each person are those under which they must prevail and do their own self-work. No one can truly or successfully follow another person's path. This is even more so throughout such times of great transition, and during the "threshold moment" as I feel we are now collectively experiencing on this planet.

Such threshold moments, as I refer to them, have occurred often during the long course of life on this planet. They have occurred through natural catastrophes as well as through moments or events of great historical turmoil. There is, it seems, a connection between geological events, a sense of prescient knowing or prophecy, and the psychic state of humankind that coalesce or converge to form periods of great planetary change. J.G. Bennett recognised this pattern when he stated in a 1962 lecture:

> It seems to me that this does suggest three converging lines of evidence: one, the geological and climatological scientific evidence that strange things are happening within the earth; prodigious strains have been set up on the surface of the earth that may result in quite big tectonic shifts, big movements of the earth surface ... The second is the convergence of prediction that something very important is to happen on earth before the end of this century. And the third that is again different. It is just what you and I and all of us can see for ourselves about the present unnatural state of mankind.[2]

Great events or happenings rarely occur in isolation. And when an event is set to impact the psychic state of humankind across the planet, there is greater likelihood that it corresponds to other "big movements of the earth surface". There is an overwhelming sense among many people that some great event is currently in gestation, and that it is manifesting (or bursting through) in various ways that may appear on a surface level to be random when in reality they are all connected beneath as part of an unfolding phenomenon. The global media tend to report upon the separated events and occurrences as though they are aspects of a fragmented picture, like pointing at the various mountain peaks while ignoring the connected land mass that sustains them. Yet the bigger picture is one of a great correspondence that is in process. This is perhaps why the minority of those who wield material, outer power are desperate to consolidate this into a centralised control structure in a deluded attempt to benefit, and remain in power afterwards, from the coming transformative changes set to unfold upon the planet. Human civilisation is presently moving through a dangerous zone—a liminal zone—as it deals with the energetics of upheaval involved in the reorganisation and resettlement of human life.

The final outcome of this reshuffle, I deeply suspect, is one that shall lead to a psychic revolution within humankind. Because of this, authoritarian elements within the human power structure are desperate to forestall this inevitable process by introducing artificial components into the structuring of human life on the planet (as this book has discussed). Again, I quote from the insights of J. G. Bennett, who more than seventy years ago perceived this transitional state for humankind:

> This is one reason why the change—the transition period from one epoch to another, from one world to another—is a dangerous period. Old ideas have lost their momentum and can no longer move the world. New ideas have not yet gained momentum. All through history, and even before the beginning of history, we find such periods accompanied by war and revolution; not because war and revolution are inevitable in themselves, but because people have lacked that discrimination which would enable them to use this situation rightly. If we are able to go into a world in which this is understood, then the course of history can be different, because the destiny of all mankind can be raised to a higher level. There is no higher purpose in the life of man than to bring about this great transition.[3]

It is in the final stage of a grand cycle that the world reaches its "extremity of separation" from its Source. As it is a period of remoteness from correspondence with the sacred, so it is a time of disorientation and distortion, which brings with it a mad rush for attaining power. In this period between epochs there is a greater fluidity, and uncertainty, within social-cultural structures and systems. And it is within this very space of uncertainty, before the "new ideas" have gained momentum, where particular forces are most likely to intervene to exploit the situation towards a direction that favours their aims and agenda. And this is what we are witnessing now through a globalising arrangement of "old order" power strategies. In order to gain dominance at this time, the power strategies are needing to foster an energetic environment of separation, fragmentation, and splintering. That is, physically, emotionally, and psychologically, people, communities, groups, and nations, are being divided against themselves and others through a range of polarising agendas. These agendas, some of which have been discussed in this book, include self, sexual, political, racial, and sociocultural identities. And much of this has been orchestrated through the digital architecture of techno-materialism. Also, through eliciting a desired behaviour or outcome by way of *choice architecture*, which provides "nudges" to steer people and groups into specific behaviour and actions.[4]

The fragmentation of the human psyche, much of which is being achieved through covert methods of mass behaviour modification, serves to strip a person of their contact with essence or *being*. Hence, the state of not-being, which has been referred to throughout this book, is an energetic "dark mode" that keeps people, groups, and communities within a lower resonant frequency; and hence, more susceptible to further manipulations. Direct and/or *essential* contact between people, between our environment, and between non-material or metaphysical realms, has been diminishing for a long time. And now, it has reached its lowest point—a place of deep separation and fragmentation. And it is this place of deep alienation that is being exploited by a ruling minority to further usher (or herd) people into a controlled commons—a corral or enclosure—that is monitored and managed by artificial programs. At the same time, the imminence of an end of an age, an era, brings with it a sense of otherworldliness. There is greater metaphysical or "otherworldly" energy available at transition or threshold moments, as if the veil thins to allow a penetration, a mergence, of energies. And the approach to such a major threshold, as is occurring now, can also be referred to as *apocalyptic*.

Apocalyptic times

The term *apocalypse* comes from ancient Greek (ἀποκάλυψις—apokálypsis) which literally means "from cover"; that is, a disclosure or revelation of great significance (or knowledge). In religious terminology it has been used to denote a disclosure of something very important that was previously hidden or unknown. This may refer to some "heavenly secrets", or similar divine disclosures that might bring understanding into earthly life. Here we have a term representing a "revelation of the veiled". During, or as the consequence of, an apocalypse we have individual and/or collective revelation of some hidden or veiled knowledge or understanding. This is in contradistinction to the related term Armageddon. Armageddon in ancient Greek is Ἁρμαγεδών, Harmagedōn (and in Hebrew is Har Məgīddō) which is the prophesied location of a battle during the "end times". The term *Armageddon* is used in a general sense to refer to any "end of the world" scenario. Yet it has no revelatory significance or suggests any epiphany. It refers to a physical battle, a time of great end times war—the "war to end all wars". These two terms are not equal but represent distinct phenomena: one is an instance of revelation (apocalypse), while the other is a specific physical "war to end all wars" (Armageddon). These terms signify different narrative timelines. One is an unfoldment of new revelatory understanding and insight (a perceptual awakening). The other functions on a distinctly physical level that brings people into a timeline of physical warfare, disruption, and destruction (material entanglement).

Moreover, the *apocalypse* perspective indicates a movement towards something. Through revelation there is a sense of transitioning towards something, whether this be perceptual awareness or a new mode of comprehension. On the other hand, the *Armageddon* mode more likely suggests a running away from something, such as running away from the destruction and devastation of war. These different narrative positionings provide an energetic environment for their adherents; that is, a particular reality construct. And, we should be warned, reality has a funny way of responding to what's on our mind. What we are running away from usually meets us head on, at some point. Just like in those abstract dreams where we are attempting to run away from some fear but are going nowhere. The apocalypse-revelation mode, to call it as such, suggests a position of receptiveness and openness to unknown potentials. There is uncertainty, for sure, yet with an inner sense of trust. And this ultimately works in our favour, for we cannot run away from ourselves no matter how fast or how hard we try. We can take ourselves to an underground bunker, or to some isolated island—yet we *take ourselves* with us. And with ourselves, as if moved by the invisible hands of an unseen realm, we are approaching a significant threshold for humanity and human civilisation upon this planet. And the only thing that stands in the way, obscuring our view, is the web of techno-materialism that is being spun by the spindly fingers of an authoritarian, technocratic minority.

Indications have been given that a non-material, or *supersensory*, force is entering into our physical domain. And as its arrival accelerates, it is set to bring about great changes. Earthly history, it has been said, is but a shadow of the greater influences under which it materially exists.

There are influences which change the course of events that cannot be reduced to cause and effect. Their origin lies apart from the material realm, and yet they operate through matter-reality. And it may be that under the remit of such influences the earthly domain is being set up to receive some serious shocks that will enable a specific transitional phase to be accomplished. Without such shocks, arranged in a precise manner, earthly and human evolution may sink into a period of stagnation and miss its developmental goals. It may be that because of the need for such shocks, as a trigger for revelatory phenomena to unfold, this time period receives its "apocalyptic" character:

> It is precisely this tragic *dilemma of the human consciousness* which makes the apocalyptic character of the present age. Our souls are under the spell of materialistic habits of thought. For a long time the consciousness of humanity has been concentrated on the outside of the world. Now the spiritual world is reaching humankind; humanity is arriving at the threshold; new realities overwhelm us for which no understanding is available. It must seem hopeless ever to grasp them with conscious thought. And everything depends upon whether humanity rises to that level of consciousness on which what is actually happening can be understood.[5]

Aspects that signify a "new reality" may overwhelm us, for which we have as yet few terms of reference or comprehension in which to frame them or place them into our context of reality. Hence, human perception of what "reality" is for us will need to shift so as to accommodate the new orientation of thought and perspective. And this necessary shift shall form part of a passage through the threshold of transition. For some people, this may occur without much conscious thought on their behalf, if their orientation of *being* or *essence* is already aligned with a fundamental honesty and innate connection to human goodness. Such people as these will form the "silent passengers" on this voyage where a rising tide, so to speak, will lift many of the boats in the harbour.

However, for the conscious participants who are actively seeking an engagement in the process, conscious choices will have to be taken in allowing for a transformation of their whole being during the passing of the threshold. And such people will act as forerunners within this epochal transition. For those who cling to the ruins of a lower vibratory, materialistic world, the crossing will be rough and leaking boats are

likely to find their refuge only on the sea floor. Theologian and anthro-
posophist Emil Bock states that the *Apocalypse of St. John* helps people to
think in terms of cycles:

> In order to establish and safeguard the cosmic dimensions of the
> Apocalypse we must endeavour to read in its calendar of cycles
> not only the sequence of civilizations, but also that of the plan-
> etary cycles of evolution of the earth itself. If we refer the stages
> of the Apocalypse to the very largest evolutionary cycles, then the
> seventh trumpet reveals how the whole earth-aeon of humanity
> comes to an end.[6]

Furthermore, according to Bock, the apocalypse which marks the close
of the current cycle or earth-aeon will give us a choice of crossing the
threshold or clinging more tightly to the material world. Also, as part
of the "apocalypse"—or rather, the cyclical transition—access to greater
knowledge beyond our present limitations will be necessary. Receptivity and access to expanding realms of awareness will become a feature
of the unfolding process. Yet it is likely to be uneven.

This demarcation between those who are receptive to such awareness
and those who are more materially orientated will become much more
apparent and noticeable in the times ahead. Partly, this will be because
the fraud, deceit, manipulations, and deceptions that have been an
intrinsic part of the tech-materialistic age (the technocratic tyranny) will
be more transparent to the world. This also aligns with chapter (surah)
ninety-nine from the Quran—Al-Zalzalah (Arabic: الزلزلة, al-zalzalah,
meaning: "The Quake")—where it is written:

> When the earth is shaken to her (utmost) convulsion
> And the earth throws up her burdens (from within)
> And man cries (distressed): "What is the matter with it?"
> On that Day will she declare her tidings
> For that thy Lord will have given her inspiration
> On that Day will men proceed in companies sorted out, to be
> shown the deeds that they (had done)
> Then shall anyone who has done an atom's weight of good,
> see it!
> And anyone who has done an atom's weight of evil, shall
> see it.

The shaking and convulsions of the earth (earthquakes), added to the "throwing up" from within (volcanic eruptions), alludes to the geophysical shocks that seem to accompany many cyclical transitions between epochs. And as part of the transformative nature of these epochal transitions, the transparency of dark deeds and the purification of the shadows seem core aspects. However, we should not forget the fundamental issue here—the nature of human consciousness and perception.

It is not another industrial revolution that we seek but a psychic revolution. All the external focus upon a Fourth Industrial Revolution (the dream of a global elitist corporatocracy) is both a distraction and a clever strategy that strengthens the technocratic agenda. The organic evolutionary path, however, requires a revolution of internal matters: an expansion of psychic faculties and cognitive perception. The limitations of our present material paradigm are that it assumes that the current stage of a non-visionary consciousness is the normal and only possible one. As such, visionary material is often regarded either literally and dogmatically or rejected as being mere allegory with no inner or substantial meaning. And yet, there is such material as pervades our cultures and historical landscape—whether in sacred texts, designs, monuments, and other mediums—that have their origin in a higher realm. As such, their true meaning can only be interpreted from the state of expanded cognitive perception (what is often loosely referred to as "higher consciousness"). That which belongs to a "higher realm" may now be increasingly flowing into the physical world of the human being. In other words, the "grace" enters from above (non-material realm) and works down into the body and into the material world. The hubris of the material world, with its aims for transhumanism and an AI god, is replicating the folly of the Tower of Babel which, as in a reverse or inverted manner, was trying to reach from the ground up towards the sacred realm. This artificial material construction built upon a united language (aka "global order"), was recognised as a travesty and thus fragmented into confusion. Similarly, the techno-materialist folly is to redefine the sacred path through a non-organic or silicon trajectory; that is, through an artificial body and machinic mind. This substitution of the sacred opposes the natural development of new organs of perception beyond the present five senses. The genuine spiritualising of the organic body is simultaneously a humanising of it.

The transhuman or machinic direction is a path of material progress yet one that is further distanced from the evolutionary goals of humankind (a trajectory that is aligned with cosmic or universal goals). In this sense, the human evolutionary journey is a form of quest. This idea of the "quest" has been an intrinsic part of human history, folklore, mythology, and cultural heritage from time immemorial. The notion of a quest has been engrained in many cultures, although today is less established in modern societies. The questing path has underpinned the foundations of the human journey. The quest also recognises the process of purification and regeneration—of trial and error—and the eventual triumph over struggle and strife. It also suggests that a minimal degree of preparation and fortitude is required, for the notion of the quest is a *potentialisation of the human condition*. First, we need to see ourselves for who we really are, rather than running ahead of ourselves to transform the human condition into that of a techno-slave. What is required as we collectively approach the threshold is transformative change; that is, to transfigure the human "being" rather than just concentrating on the body and personality. This makes the difference between a world of ideas and a world with transfigured beings. The techno-materialist path only accumulates—it does not utilise its resources for transmutation. It only collects more and more and ultimately burdens itself with external entanglements.

The threshold compels us to "spiritualise intelligence" which is contrary to the materialist notion of containment by artificial intelligence. Artificial intelligence and the "will to technology" have become the semi-religious doctrine and dogma of hyper-materialism that is based on entropy. Such entropic forces push and pull towards the final decay of all material things including life and the universe (and everything in between). Allegiance to an entropic path is a form of slavery. As J. G. Bennett states: "… the greatest tragedy of modern man is his inner slavery, which is ten thousand times worse than outer slavery."[7] Inner slavery comes through a lack and laziness within people, and an over-reliance upon external, material devices and conveniences. Instead of having faith and hope that a person can change by making real effort, too many people are entertained with illusions that then take them away from the impulse to make any real change within themselves. The external gaze is occupied with the development of external techniques, hardly realising that the more important work is to discover the techniques for changing oneself. It is not only about the liberation of oneself from a life of automation and technocracy; it is a question of how a changed person can newly live an effective outer life. Encountering the threshold will have great impact on many levels and will be experienced in accordance with the inner state of each individual. There is no getting around it or avoiding it. We are now being forced to look beyond programmed exteriors and to truly see, perceive, and intuit what is real for us, and how to live meaningfully in this world. The outer materialistic gaze is looking away from the "real" and this leads to involution—to stagnation, entropy, and decay. The process of evolutionary development is assisted when the human gaze turns around to look back towards the Origin—towards a direct perception of the real. If we forget ourselves, become lazy and unaware, and allow ourselves to be carried along by techno-materialistic forces—the stream of involution—then we are not only denying our origin but rejecting the very reason of our existence. It is easier to be carried along by the path of involution, for real effort is required to align with evolutionary developmental goals. Yet, to take the easy path will eventually lead into a developmental dead end.

The present epoch is coming to its inevitable end-phase, or transition, as it approaches a civilisational threshold. The present is therefore closing down, and its systems, structures, and modes of thinking are perishing. We can choose to perish with it and become an artefact of the past. Or we can choose to push through into a new phase of creative development. This future is open and must be met in the right way. If we ignore or deny it, then we only deceive ourselves and continue to remain within a false pretence of life. We can embrace what awaits us, in the correct manner and state of beingness. Or we can stand back and watch the expected collapse of what we remain clinging to. While there will inevitably be external conflicts and confrontations upon the world stage, we should also be mindful that there will be confrontations between those who have a degree of knowledge and awareness and those who do not. And later, there may also be a confrontation between those with this awareness and those who will have to gain awareness whether it is their choice or not. These conflicts will largely be internal ones. There is a part within most people that does not wish to know of such things, although they may secretly feel such possibility. Yet there will come a time when people can no longer ignore such internal truths, and they will have to face the veil of ignorance that has clothed them for so many of their earthly years. For what appears external to humanity is really that which is inside. And this shall become the contestation between those of *being* and those of *not-being*. And this clash shall become the true underpinnings of the revelation to come. One way or another, each person will come to a choice point regarding their sense of self and beingness.

* * *

The final word is this: Humanity has reached a moment in its long journey where it can finally participate in the processes of its own evolution and development. Not for thousands of years has there been such a need for people (who are able) to consciously participate in the crossing of a "threshold". The reason for this is that the transition from one epoch to another requires a minimum of conscious effort and awareness. And it is this call for conscious awareness that shall close this book. The time has come (now that we are aware of the ills of our current civilisation) to focus on the efforts required for a successful passing of the threshold that presently faces us, and which is unfolding around us as we speak. A little self-awareness from each capable individual will be the minimal price of admission to the crossing of the waters ...

> *Neither ancient occultism nor modern science will serve to satisfy the deepest need of the humanity of the future, the need to establish a link between the human soul and spiritual revelation*
> —Rudolf Steiner (August 18, 1911, Munich)

Notes

1. J. G. Bennett, *Lectures on Gurdjieff: 14 Public Lectures, 1949–1973 (The Collected Works of J. G. Bennett Book 45)* (Petersham, MA: The J. G. Bennett Foundation, 2020), 132.
2. J. G. Bennett, *Natural Catastrophes That Change History: A series of four public lectures, 1962 (The Collected Works of J. G. Bennett Book 51)* (Petersham, MA: The J. G. Bennett Foundation, 2024), 107–108.
3. J. G. Bennett, *Lectures on Gurdjieff: 14 Public Lectures, 1949–1973 (The Collected Works of J. G. Bennett Book 45)* (Petersham, MA: The J. G. Bennett Foundation, 2020), 27.
4. Shoshana Zuboff, *The Age of Surveillance Capitalism: The Fight for a Human Future at the New Frontier of Power* (London: Profile Books, 2019).
5. Emil Bock, *The Apocalypse of St. John* (Edinburgh, UK: Floris Books, 2005), 88.

6. Emil Bock, *The Apocalypse of St. John* (Edinburgh, UK: Floris Books, 2005), 196.

7. J. G. Bennett, *Talks on Beelzebub's Tales* (York Beach, ME.: Samuel Weiser, 1988), 9.

POSTSCRIPT

In this book I've been discussing how the forces of techno-materialism are attempting to persuade humankind that the material world is the only world; that there are no sacred or metaphysical elements at all, and that through materialism human beings can create a worldly paradise. It's a temptation for many people. And although it is ultimately a failed project, it may make sufficient damage along the way.

In many areas of life, humans have demonstrated that they have cleverness without wisdom; thinking without conscience; and behaviours without correct intention. If we are not careful, the world we inhabit will calcify through a rigidity of technology rather than creating genuine advancement through liberating technologies. If our technologies are utilised for self-indulgence instead of self-development, then humans will inevitably degenerate. Knowledge must be combined with awareness. We must neither lose the world, nor lose ourselves in it. There are influences creating apathy among humans, and this often culminates in a rejection and denial of what we may loosely term as "spiritual" impulses. Yet as I stated at the outset, recognition of the adversary is the beginning of our conquest of it.

What I have discussed in this book is the approach to a "threshold" and the forces that are vying for dominance in a techno-material future *this side* of the threshold, and thus a denial or blockage of those meta-physical forces wishing to aid humanity to perceive and comprehend reality *beyond* the threshold. Various wisdom traditions have their own understanding of this threshold, and they speak of forces that are guarding it from both sides. That is, protecting the unprepared or mal-intentioned on this side from penetrating through it, as well as guard-ing those forces from beyond the current threshold from inadvertently passing into the material realm. In other words, passage operates both ways. It is to our benefit to be receptive to the incoming metaphysical impulses that are aligned with the genuine evolutionary development of humankind.

It has also been said that beyond the threshold lies wisdom—*Sophia*—and with her comes creative imagination and inspiration. It is precisely this creative imagination and inspiration that has been "stolen" or atrophied by those forces actively dominant in the material realm. We can see this clearly through the processes of automation and not-being that have been explored throughout this book. These deadening or cal-cifying forces that are emphasised through technocracy are opposing the living energies of creative imagination and inspiration. This is the representation of the will-to-technology that I have discussed, which is inverse to the will-to-revelation that lies with sophianic wisdom beyond the threshold. It is these impulses of revelation, I speculate, that are attempting to penetrate the material realm to inspire those of human-kind who are open and receptive to such elements. A part of these forces of inspiration is the power to recognise objective truth. And objective truth carries with it a magical force—a creative force. These "magical" impulses are also what we may recognise as metaphysical. Wisdom and light await us beyond the threshold. A techno-material world running on sub-natural light (electricity) is pulling us back.

Our cosmos is not an abode of dark matter. It is a magical realm of creative and intelligent light. And it is towards the light of truth and wisdom that we must turn.

REFERENCES

Agamben, Giorgio (1998). *Homo Sacer: Sovereign Power and Bare Life*. Redwood City, CA: Stanford University Press.

Agamben, Giorgio (2005). *State of Exception*. Chicago, IL: Chicago University Press.

Agamben, Giorgio (2009). *What Is an Apparatus & Other Essays*. Redwood City, CA: Stanford University Press.

Allen, Joe (2023). *Dark Aeon: Transhumanism and the War Against Humanity*. New York: War Room Books.

Arendt, Hannah (1978). *The Life of the Mind*. New York: Houghton Mifflin Harcourt.

Barks, Coleman & Moyne, John (Trans.) (1995). *The Essential Rumi*. New York: Harper.

Baudrillard, Jean (1994). *The Illusion of the End*. Cambridge: Polity Press.

Baudrillard, Jean (2008). *The Perfect Crime*. London: Verso.

Bennett, J. G. (1988). *Talks on Beelzebub's Tales*. York Beach, ME: Samuel Weiser.

Bennett, J. G. (2020). *Lectures on Gurdjieff: 14 Public Lectures, 1949–1973 (The Collected Works of J. G. Bennett Book 45)*. Petersham, MA: The J. G. Bennett Foundation.

Bennett, J. G. (2024). *Natural Catastrophes That Change History: A series of four public lectures, 1962 (The Collected Works of J. G. Bennett Book 51)*. Petersham, MA: The J. G. Bennett Foundation.

Bock, Emil (2005). *The Apocalypse of St. John*. Edinburgh, UK: Floris Books.

Bondarev, G. A. (1993). *Crisis of Civilization*. London: Wellspring Bookshop.

Collin, Rodney (1956). *The Theory of Eternal Life*. London: Vincent Stuart Publishers.

Crick, Francis (1981). *Life Itself: Its Origin and Nature*. New York: Simon & Schuster.

Dennis, Kingsley L. (2021). *Hijacking Reality: The Reprogramming & Reorganization of Human Life*. Leicester, UK: Beautiful Traitor Books.

Dennis, Kingsley L. (2023). *The Inversion: How We Have Been Tricked into Perceiving a False Reality*. London: Aeon Books.

Desmet, Mattias (2022). *The Psychology of Totalitarianism*. White River Junction, VT: Chelsea Green Publishing Co.

Foucault, Michel (1979). *Discipline and Punish: The Birth of the Prison*. London: Vintage.

Fromm, Erich (1955). *The Sane Society*. London: Routledge, 2002.

Gruwez, Christine (2014). *Mani & Rudolf Steiner*. Great Barrington, MA: SteinerBooks.

Guenon, Rene (2004a). *The Crisis of the Modern World*. Hillsdale, NY: Sophia Perennis.

Guenon, Rene (2004b). *The Reign of Quantity and the Signs of the Times*. Hillsdale, NY: Sophia Perennis.

Harari, Yuval Noah (2018). *21 Lessons for the 21st Century*. London: Jonathan Cape.

Havel, Vaclav (1985). *The Power of the Powerless: Citizens Against the State in Central Eastern Europe*. London: Routledge.

Jonas, Hans (1958). *The Gnostic Religion: The Message of the Alien God & the Beginnings of Christianity*. Boston, MA: Beacon Press.

Kroker, Arthur (2003). *The Will to Technology and the Culture of Nihilism: Heidegger, Marx, and Nietzsche*. Toronto, Canada: University of Toronto Press.

Kroker, Arthur (2014). *Exits to the Posthuman Future*. Cambridge: Polity Press.

Łobaczewski, Andrew (2007). *Political Ponerology: A Science on the Nature of Evil Adjusted for Political Purposes*. Otto, NC: Red Pill Press.

McGilchrist, Iain (2010). *The Master and His Emissary: The Divided Brain and the Making of the Western World*. New Haven, CT: Yale University Press.

Merton, Thomas (1957). *The Silent Life*. London: Burns & Oates.

Misra, Bibhu Dev (2023). *Yuga Shift: The End of the Kali Yuga & The Impending Planetary Transformation*. Ajitgarh, India: White Falcon Publishing.

Moravec, Hans (1988). *Mind Children: The Future of Robot & Human Intelligence*. Cambridge, MA: Harvard University Press.

Mumford, Lewis (1967). *The Myth of the Machine: Technics and Human Development*. New York: Secker & Warburg.

Mumford, Lewis (1970). *The Myth of the Machine: The Pentagon of Power*. New York: Harcourt Brace.

Nestfield-Cookson, Bernard (1998). *Michael and the Two-Horned Beast: The Challenge of Evil Today in the Light of Rudolf Steiner's Science of the Spirit*. Forest Row, UK: Temple Lodge Publishing.

Pearson, Keith Ansell (1997). *Viroid Life: Perspectives on Nietzsche and the Transhuman Condition*. London: Routledge.

Rose, Seraphim (1994). *Nihilism: The Root of the Revolution of the Modern Age*. Platina, CA: St. Herman of Alaska Brotherhood, 2018.

Selg, Peter (2022). *The Future of Ahriman and the Awakening of Souls*. Forest Row, UK: Temple Lodge Publishing.

Smith, Huston (1992). *Forgotten Truth: The Common Vision of the World's Religions*. New York: HarperCollins.

Stegmann, Carl (1997). *The Other America*. Fair Oaks, CA: Rudolf Steiner College Press.

Steiner, Rudolf (1997). *EVIL: Selected Lectures by Rudolf Steiner*. Forest Row, UK: Rudolf Steiner Press.

Steiner, Rudolf (2015). *Problems of Society: An Esoteric View: From Luciferic Past to Ahrimanic Future*. Forest Row, UK: Rudolf Steiner Press.

Tarnas, Richard (2006). *Cosmos and Psyche: Intimations of a New World View*. London: Penguin.

Upton, Charles (2005). *Legends of the End: Prophecies of the End Times, Antichrist, Apocalypse, and Messiah from Eight Religious Traditions*. Hillsdale, NY: Sophia Perennis.

Versluis, Arthur (2023). *American Gnosis: Political Religion and Transcendence*. Oxford: Oxford University Press.

Vervaeke, J., Miscevic, F., & Mastropietro, C. (2017). *Zombies in Western Culture: A Twenty-First Century Crisis*. Cambridge: Open Book Publishers.

Waterfield, Robin (2017). *Rene Guenon and the Future of the West: The Life and Writings of a 20th-Century Metaphysician*. Hillsdale, NY: Sophia Perennis.

Wiener, Norbert (1964). *God & Golem, Inc.: A Comment on Certain Points Where Cybernetics Impinges on Religion*. Cambridge, MA: MIT Press.

Wilson, Colin (2018). *The Age of Defeat*. London: Aristeia Press.

Zuboff, Shoshana (2019). *The Age of Surveillance Capitalism: The Fight for a Human Future at the New Frontier of Power*. London: Profile Books.

ABOUT THE AUTHOR

KINGSLEY L. DENNIS, PhD, is a full-time writer and researcher. He is the author of over thirty books including *The Inversion: How We Have Been Tricked into Perceiving a False Reality; UNIFIED: Cosmos, Life, Purpose; Hijacking Reality; Healing the Wounded Mind; The Modern Seeker; Bardo Times; Breaking the Spell; The Struggle for your Mind; New Consciousness for a New World*, and *Dawn of the Akashic Age* (with Ervin Laszlo). Kingsley also runs his own publishing imprint, Beautiful Traitor Books (www.beautifultraitorbooks.com), where he has published non-fiction, fiction, children's books, essays, and poetry. Most of his work can be found at his Substack page: https://kingsleyldennis.substack.com/. His personal website is: www.kingsleydennis.com.

INDEX